The Church on Lafayette Square
A History of St. John's Church, Washington, D.C.

1815 · 1970

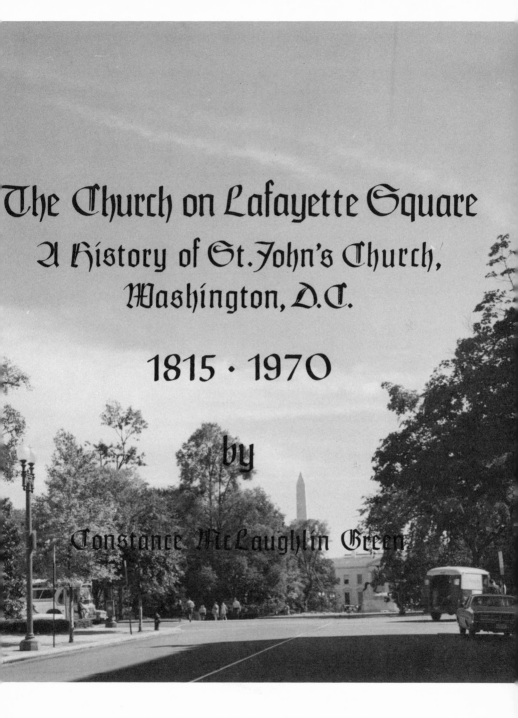

The Church on Lafayette Square
A History of St. John's Church, Washington, D.C.

1815 · 1970

by

Constance McLaughlin Green

POTOMAC BOOKS, INC., PUBLISHERS
1518 K Street, N.W.
Washington, D.C. 20005

Printed in the United States of America
by McGregor & Werner, Inc.
Washington, D.C.

Library of Congress Catalog Number 78-141034
Standard Book Numbers 0-87107-016-2 (Cloth) and 0-87107-017-0 (Paper)

PREFACE

As the life of St. John's unfolds in the pages following, one is ineluctably led into the mainstream of historic moments in our country's past. Born in a time of stress, St. John's in many ways mirrors the trials and tribulations which beset the country in its early years. Equally it reflects the strengths and dynamic drives which have brought America to its present position of power and responsibility.

Located since 1815 across Lafayette Square from the White House, St. John's never had a chance to become a self-satisfied little parish. The turbulent and exciting events of an emerging nation all had their impact on the life and style of the parish. As Washington became more and more the focal point of world political power, so did the responsibilities of St. John's expand to minister adequately to the men and women who made up its ever more diverse membership.

The pages of this book give the reader a strong sense that the challenges and difficulties of each succeeding decade have been met and dealt with wisely if not perfectly by its clergy, wardens and vestries. From the outset it is clear that St. John's continually sought ways of helping less fortunate individuals outside its immediate purview. At the turn of this century, Dr. Roland Cotton Smith was expressing in his sermons the direction in which he believed St. John's should be heading. In effect he said that the Church is not safe if all men are speaking well of it. It will be true to itself only if instead of seeking popularity it is championing some cause that has not yet been won.

More than sixty years later our present rector, Dr. John C. Harper, reinforces this philosophy as he quoted from *Pilgrims' Progress* in a recent report to the parish: "I must venture. To go back is nothing but death; to go forward is fear of death and life everlasting beyond it. I will yet go forward."

To those of us who are fortunate enough to be regular worshipers at St. John's today, there is a constant awareness of its rare beauty and rich tradition while at the same time there is an inescapable challenge not merely to preserve this beauty and tradition but more importantly to make it sensitive and inspiring to this generation and to those that will follow.

August 1, 1970

Philip H. Watts
Senior Warden

Livingston T. Merchant
Junior Warden

CHRONOLOGY

June-July 1800	Transfer of the U.S. government to the new capital, Washington, D.C.
March 1801	Thomas Jefferson becomes President.
March 1809	James Madison becomes President.
April 1812	Tentative plans to build a second Episcopal church in Washington.
June 1812	U.S. declaration of war on Great Britain.
August 1814	Capture by the British of the U.S. capital and burning of the White House, the Capitol and other public buildings.
January-February 1815	Signing of the Peace Treaty; U.S. Senate votes to keep the capital in Washington.
July-September 1815	Purchase of a site on the "President's Square" for the new church and selection of Benjamin Henry Latrobe as architect.
September 14, 1815	Laying of the cornerstone of the church.
July 1816	Election of the first vestry.
October 27, 1816	Celebration of the first service at St. John's.
November 1816	Appointment of the Reverend William Wilmer as the first rector, and offer of a free pew to President Madison.
December 27, 1816	St. John's Day, consecration of the church.
March 1817	Inauguration of President James Monroe.
April 1817	Installation of the Reverend William Hawley as second rector.
Summer 1820-July 1822	Enlargement of the church building, and construction of a belfry equipped with a bronze bell.
1824-1825	Visits of General Lafayette to the United States and the subsequent renaming of the President's Square to "Lafayette Square".
March 1825	John Quincy Adams becomes President.
March 1829	Andrew Jackson becomes President.
August 1835	First race riots in Washington.
March-April 1841	President William Henry Harrison dies and is succeeded by John Tyler.
October-November 1842	Rearrangement and redecoration of the church's interior.
January-March 1845	Death of the Reverend William Hawley, and installation of the Reverend Smith Pyne as rector.
March 1845	James K. Polk becomes President.
December 1848-September 1850	Congressional debates on permitting slavery in the territories acquired from Mexico and "The Compromise" of 1850.
March 1849-July 1850	President Zachary Taylor dies and is succeeded by Millard Fillmore.
March 1853	Franklin Pierce becomes President.
March 1857	James Buchanan becomes President.
February-April 1861	Formation of The Confederate States of America, the firing on Fort Sumner, and President Lincoln's first call for volunteers.
March 1861	Inauguration of Abraham Lincoln as President.

April 1862	Emancipation of slaves in the District of Columbia.
January 1863	Lincoln's Emancipation Proclamation.
April 9, 1865	Lee's surrender at Appomattox.
April 14, 1865	Assassination of President Lincoln; succeeded by Andrew Johnson.
September 1865	Installation of the Reverend John Vaughan Lewis as fourth rector of St. John's.
November 1866-1867	Opening of a biracial Home and Mission House and the founding of St. Mary's Chapel.
January 1867	Congressional act franchising adult Negro males in the District of Columbia.
July 1868	Passage of the 14th Amendment to the Constitution.
March 1869	Ulysses S. Grant becomes President.
June 1869	Passage of the first civil rights ordinance by Washington's city council.
October 1870	Opening of St. John's Hospital for Children.
September 1873	Beginning of a five-year country-wide depression.
June 1874	Disenfranchisement of all citizens of the District of Columbia and substitution of rule by Congress and presidentially-appointed commissioners.
March 1877	James A. Garfield becomes President.
1878	Conversion of bankrupt St. John's Hospital into St. John's Orphanage.
March 1881	Installation of the Reverend William Andrew Leonard as rector of St. John's.
September 1881	Assassination of President Garfield; succeeded by Chester A. Arthur.
1883	Remodelling of St. John's under the aegis of James Renwick and the introduction of stained glass windows made by the curator of glass at Chartres Cathedral.
March 1885	Grover Cleveland becomes President.
March 1889	Benjamin Harrison becomes President.
November 1889	The installation of the Reverend George Douglas as rector.
1892	Installation of the Reverend Alexander Mackay-Smith as rector.
January 1893	Chartering of National Cathedral Foundation by Congress.
March 1893	Grover Cleveland returns as President.
October 1893-1894	Onset of a severe world-wide depression, and the appearance of Coxey's "Army of the Unemployed" in Washington.
March 1897	William McKinley becomes President.
September 14, 1901	Assassination of President McKinley; succeeded by Theodore Roosevelt.
December 1902	Installation of the Reverend Roland Cotton Smith as rector of St. John's.
March 1909	William Howard Taft becomes President.
March 1913	Woodrow Wilson becomes President.
January 1917	Celebration of St. John's centennial.
April 6, 1917	U.S. declaration of war.
November 11, 1918	Armistice ends World War I.
June 28, 1919	Signing of the Treaty of Versailles.
July 1919	Race riot in Washington.
March 19, 1920	Senate rejection of unqualified adherence of U.S. to the League of Nations.
1920	Parish committee's appraisal of the successes and failures of St. John's.

March 1921-August 1923	President Warren G. Harding dies and is succeeded by Calvin Coolidge.
January 1922	Installation of the Reverend Robert Johnston as rector.
1927	Beginning of the French services at St. John's.
March 1929	Herbert Hoover becomes President.
October 1929	Stock market crash and the beginning of the "Great Depression".
June-July 1932	"Bonus March" on Washington.
March-June 1933	"First 100 Days" of the New Deal under President Franklin D. Roosevelt.
July 1934	Installation of the Reverend Oliver James Hart as rector of St. John's.
July 1940	Installation of the Reverend Charles Leslie Glenn as rector.
December 7, 1941	Pearl Harbor and U.S. declaration of war.
January 1942	Dr. Glenn's call to active duty as Navy chaplain.
April 12, 1945-August 1945	Death of President Roosevelt; succeeded by Harry S. Truman. VE and VJ Days.
November 1945-December 1955	Return of Dr. Glenn to St. John's; recognition of voting rights for women at parish meetings; acquisition of a new parish house; and minor remodelling of the church.
January 20, 1953	Dwight D. Eisenhower becomes President.
1956-1957	Closing of St. John's Orphanage, opening of St. John's Development Center for Children, and the installation of the Reverend Donald Mayberry as rector.
January 20, 1961	John F. Kennedy becomes President.
March 10, 1963	Installation of the Reverend John C. Harper as rector.
August 1963	March on Washington under the leadership of the Reverend Martin Luther King, Jr.
November 12, 1963	Assassination of President John F. Kennedy; succeeded by Lyndon B. Johnson.
April-September 1965	Celebration of the Sesquicentennial of St. John's with organ concerts and a symposium on "Church and City".
March 1966	"Operation Outreach" begins with grant to Anacostia's Chapel of St. Philip the Evangelist.
1966-1970	Outreach programs expanded by new work at Star of Bethlehem Church, Kingman Boys' Club, development of training programs.
April 1968	Washington riots following assassination of Dr. Martin Luther King, Jr.
January 20, 1969	Inauguration of President Richard M. Nixon.
Spring 1969	"The Three Year Program" campaign raises over $800,000 in pledges; new Gress-Miles organ installed and chancel renovated.
October 15, 1969	Moratorium against the Viet Nam war; former Justice Arthur Goldberg speaks to convocation of lawyers in St. John's Church.
Spring 1970	Parish begins investment outreach program by placing $80,000 of endowment funds in inner city investment programs.

ILLUSTRATIONS

TABLE OF CONTENTS

CONSTANCE MCLAUGHLIN GREEN received the Pulitzer prize for History in 1963 for *Washington: Village and Capital, 1800-1878.*

She was born in 1897, received an AB from Smith, an MA from Mt. Holyoke and a Ph.D. from Yale. Mrs. Green has served with the federal government and has taught history at the University of Chicago, Mt. Holyoke College, Smith College, American University, and George Washington University. She was the Commonwealth Fund Lecturer at University College, University of London.

Mrs. Green is also the author of *American Cities in the Growth of the Nation*; *Washington: Capital City, 1879-1950*; the *Rise of Urban America* and the *Secret City, A History of Race Relations in the National Capital.*

1

The First Generation Of St. John's

When residents of the Federal City who lived in the vicinity of the President's House first gave thought to forming a second Episcopal parish in Washington, the American capital was little more than a village. Its 5,200 white inhabitants of 1810 were scattered from the Eastern Branch above the Navy Yard to Rock Creek, some five miles to the northwest as the crow flies. And only a crow or the water fowl of the swampy stretches along the Potomac could cover that distance easily. In 1807 members of the then 12-year-old Washington Parish had built Christ Church on Capitol Hill, presumably because a parishioner had given a plot of land there for the purpose, but the location had drawbacks for part of the congregation. While a number of Episcopalians occupied quarters about the Marine Barracks and the Navy Yard, more lived in the neighborhood of the government's executive offices and the White House. To attend services at Christ Church meant for householders of northwest Washington an uncomfortable trip; after rains, mud clogged the roads; in hot dry spells dust choked man and beast, and at all seasons pot holes and tree stumps even along the main thoroughfare of Pennsylvania Avenue presented hazards. As this was the "city of magnificent distances," in the politely derogatory phrase of the witty Portuguese minister, the vestry of Christ Church appointed a committee in April 1812 "to obtain donations

1

for building a church in the west end of the city." Two
months later the United States declared war upon Great
Britain.

Although fighting a war against the greatest power in
Europe at first sat rather lightly upon Americans, within a
year it became a serious matter. As every able-bodied man
between the ages of 18 and 45 in the District of Columbia
was subject to militia duty, military service periodically
disrupted citizens' lives completely. During a lull in the
early months of 1814, several of the men eager to establish
a new Episcopal parish formed another committee, but
catastrophe struck the community and the nation in August. British troops marched into the capital, burned every
public building except the Patent Office, and left Washington two days later a smoking ruin. For weeks Americans
wondered whether the Union could survive at all. Several
victories put that fear to rest before the end of the year,
but residents of the capital still waited apprehensively for a
congressional decision about whether to relocate the seat of
government. Were that disaster to befall, Washington City
would shrink to a mere hamlet. Not until February 1815,
when the Senate endorsed the House of Representatives
vote to rebuild the capital on the Potomac, and when
President Madison a fortnight later signed the peace treaty,
did Washingtonians dare plan for the future. Nor even then,
with temporary accommodations to be provided for the
government, and with federal and local officials preoccu-
pied with rebuilding the public edifices, was the time yet
ripe to pursue vigorously the founding of a second Episcopal church in the city. That moment came in the summer
of 1815.

The sponsors of the projected new church were highly
respected citizens. Of the fourteen named in the earliest
notices of the proposal, Thomas H. Gillis was the most
active in initiating negotiations; he had been a member of
the original committee appointed by the Christ Church
vestry. As Chief Clerk in the Navy Accounting Office,
furthermore, he held a place of some importance in the
federal governmental hierarchy. John Graham and James
Davidson were also members of the earlier committee;
Graham was Chief Clerk to Secretary of State James

Monroe, the equivalent today of Under Secretary of State; Davidson, a devoted Mason and brother of the Grand Master of the oldest lodge in the city, was a War Department accountant. Peter Hagner, then a War Department auditor but soon to become "Watchdog of the Treasury", was at the same time father of sons destined to serve church and country as vestrymen, judge, and General of the Army. Lund Washington, a distant cousin of the first President, held a post in the Comptroller's Office of the Treasury. Thomas Munroe was President Jefferson's choice as commissioner of the federal city before mayors and elected councils came into being. John Tayloe, Virginia planter, breeder of blooded horses, and owner of the beautiful Octagon house in Washington, was probably the wealthiest of the group and one of the few who held no public office. The eminent physician, Dr. James E. Blake, was the city's war-time mayor. Three future mayors were also part of the fourteen-man committee. Joseph Gales, Jr., presided in the City Hall from 1830 to 1832; known outside Washington in 1815 as the compiler of the *Annals of Congress* and editor of the *National Intelligencer*, one of the most widely read papers in the United States, he was beloved for his personal kindnesses and his public spirit. For different reasons, John Peter Van Ness, Gales' successor as mayor, was also a notable. As affluent as he was handsome, he was president of the Bank of the Metropolis and husband of Marcia Burns, belle of the capital in the early years of the century and the heiress of her father's valuable real estate holdings in the federal city. William Winston Seaton, co-editor of the *National Intelligencer*, was to be elected mayor five times over in the 1840's. The other three original sponsors, James Thompson, Joshua Dawson, and David Easton, were lesser figures in the city of 1815.

As the solicitation of money for the new church began in earnest, members of the committee took the first steps toward their goal without waiting for formal approval from the Episcopal Convention or from the Bishop of Maryland under whose diocesan direction the new parish would fall. They purchased a plot of land to the north of the "President's Square" on H Street. Other than the blackened walls of the White House and a little farm-house at the northeast corner, no building faced on the square; a small private family graveyard occupied the southeast corner where the statue commemorating General Lafayette would stand ninety years later; an apple orchard took up most of the western half of the square. At the time, 16th Street was still a country road that cut through to the grounds of the Executive Mansion. The site of the future St. John's, in short, possessed little of the charm that would mark it a decade later, after General Lafayette's visit inspired the planting and fencing of Lafayette Square.

Having acquired a convenient location, the church sponsors engaged Benjamin Henry Latrobe to draft plans for the edifice to rise there. Latrobe, come from England to the United States in 1796 when he was 32 years old, had repeatedly demonstrated his architectural skills in his adopted country. Appointed Surveyor of Public Buildings of the United States by President Jefferson, between 1803 and 1812 he had supervised the completion of the Capitol, designed and built the south wing and central offices, and introduced in the interior halls such original decorative detail as columns with corn cob and tobacco leaf capitals instead of the conventional Corinthian acanthus leaf. In July 1815 he had returned to Washington to take charge of rebuilding the Capitol, the White House, and the other government buildings. His willingness to prepare plans for the new church ensured a handsome structure. On September 4th Thomas Gillis let a contract of $5,000 to master carpenter Richard Skinner. A few days later he contracted with Peter Morte to undertake the brick work for $6,000, a figure later raised to $6,882.52 to cover the cost of bricking the aisles and finishing the stairwell.

The laying of the cornerstone took place on September 14, 1815. Gales and Seaton published the advance notice in the *National Intelligencer,* but, unfortunately, did not describe the event when it occurred. It was a Masonic ceremony conducted by Grand Master John Davidson of the Lincoln Masonic Lodge, an office which entitled him to use the trowel with which George Washington had laid the cornerstone of the Capitol in 1793. The Reverend Alexander McCormick, rector of Christ Church, read the services that followed at Dr. James Laurie's Presbyterian

Church a few blocks away on Pennsylvania Avenue below the Treasury. Who chose the name St. John's is uncertain.

Nine months later, on May 10, 1816, a congregation of interested citizens elected trustees "to manage the secular affairs of St. John's Church until a Vestry can be appointed and apply to the Protestant Episcopal Convention for a division of the Parish of Washington." The convention granted the trustees' plea, although the bounds between the two parishes, tentatively fixed at 3rd Street just east of Judiciary Square, would not receive formal diocesan approval for another eight years. Members of the new parish elected the first vestry in July 1816: Thomas H. Gillis, Peter Hagner, John Graham, John Tayloe, John Van Ness, James Thompson, Dr. James H. Blake, and Roger C. Weightman. The vestry selected William W. Seaton and David Easton as wardens, William Parker as Register. Meanwhile the church building was nearing completion.

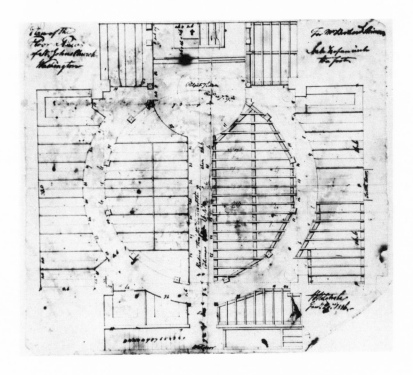

Original Floor Plan of St. John's Church by B.H. Latrobe, 1816.

Benjamin Latrobe's design bespoke the humanist rather than the mystic. Influenced by the "stripped classicism" of Cockerell and Soane, who had built the Bank of England, and by Ledoux and Vignon, architects of the Madeleine in Paris, Latrobe had nevertheless developed a distinctive style of his own. His plan for St. John's was basically a simple Greek cross, without nave, porch, or tower. Four short arms of equal length roofed over by elliptical arches formed the transepts. Where they joined the center portion of the cross stood massive pillars upon which rested a saucer-shaped dome pierced by an exquisitely proportioned cupola and lantern. Semi-lune windows at the ends of the transepts

View of St. John's from the White House.

together with the lantern afforded abundant light for day-time services. Around the church, interrupted only by the chancel on the east, ran a graceful gallery supported by a circle of slender columns. Stairs to the gallery went up to the left of the door opening out toward 16th Street. The original drawing showed the main entrance on H Street looking toward the apple orchard and the President's House beyond, but ritual called for a western entrance. Hence both. Ornamentation was restrained throughout – plain wall surfaces, few moldings, and use of recesses instead of projections. The floor was bricked, and, in the absence of a cellar and a furnace, four stoves with chimney flues in the columns near the dome heated the building after a fashion. Fifty-two high-backed box pews stood on the main floor, two of them in the chancel facing the altar, the four largest, of irregular shape curved on one side, at the ends of the aisles. The gallery held thirty-four pews and accommodated the organ over the south entrance.

As a disciple of the Enlightenment, Latrobe looked upon the congregation as a more important consideration than the ritualistic mysteries of the altar. The shallow chancel brought the altar and the simple wood communion table close to the worshippers, but the altar itself was not visible from every pew. A panel with a door in it behind the altar led to a nine-by-ten-foot vestry room. The hour-glass shaped pulpit, on the other hand, was to be seen from every seat, for it stood in front of the altar near the center of the church. The circle of the dome, the circle of the gallery, and the seven-foot circular area reserved for the pulpit clearly indicated the architect's taste for geometrical balance, just as his arrangement of altar and pulpit expressed the rationalism characteristic of the age of the Enlightenment. Simplicity marked every feature of the design. It was utterly unpretentious, but every dimension was so perfectly related to every other, every element so right, that the whole became much more than the sum of its parts. It was a thing of beauty, and Latrobe was proud of it. He refused to accept a fee for his work. He wrote his son late in 1816: "I have just completed a church that made many Washingtonians religious who had not been religious before."

The first service in the new church took place on October 27, 1816. The Reverend William H. Wilmer, rector of St. Paul's in Alexandria, officiated, as he did again at the service on the following Sunday. "It is a subject of great gratification," observed the *Intelligencer* on November 7th, "to notice the number of improvements which are embellishing our city, and we feel peculiar satisfaction in announcing the completion of the NEW EPISCOPAL CHURCH situated on an eminence opposite the President's House. The beauty of the external and the elegance of the internal arrangements combining grandeur and simplicity are well calculated to make impressions favorable to the taste of the Constructor, and to the public spirit of the citizens of Washington. The Church has already been opened to crowded congregations and only requires the appointment of a permanent pastor to complete the organization." In actuality the vestry two days before had voted to offer Mr. Wilmer the appointment. Mr. Wilmer accepted a fortnight later with "conditions," among which were his keeping his pastorate at St. Paul's and having an assistant at St. John's. Benjamin Latrobe, invited at the same time to serve as organist and choirmaster, accepted unconditionally and, at his own insistence, served without remuneration. Richard Skinner, the carpenter who had built much of the church, gladly became sexton at a salary of $100 a year.

Before arranging for the sale and rental of pews, the vestry requested Thomas Gillis and John Van Ness to wait upon the President of the United States to offer him the choice of a pew "without his being obliged to purchase the same." In acknowledging the courtesy, President Madison asked the committee to select a pew for him. They chose pew number 28, thereafter reserved in the "Church of the Presidents" for him and his White House successors. While it is probably an exaggeration to say that the founders intended St. John's to be the "Church of the Establishment," the idea was not so far-fetched in the days of the Virginia dynasty as it would have been after Congregationalist John Quincy Adams became President or Presbyterian Andrew Jackson, or the uncommitted James Polk. In December 1816 the vestry thought it proper to invite Executive Department heads and foreign ministers who were communicants of the Protestant Episcopal Church to bid for the purchase or rental of pews at the first auction. A sizable proportion of high-ranking officialdom would lend the new church prestige in the federal city and accordingly bolster parish finances. The sale and rental of pews customarily furnished the chief source of revenue for all Protestant churches of the period. At the same time the vestry offered Latrobe the free use of a pew for himself and his family, "in consideration of the high sense the Vestry entertain of his neat design of the church and of his unremitted attention to its completion, all which has been

St. John's Church and the White House, 1816.
Water color by Latrobe.

gratuitously bestowed by him." The architect declined but
said he would like "any thing as a token of their approba-
tion which he could transmit to his children." In due time
he received a suitably engraved silver goblet.

The auction of pews occurred the week before Christmas
1816. The purchase prices fixed ranged from $400 to $100,
with an annual rental dropping from $50 to $12. The
vestry must have felt disappointment at selling only four in
the first class, four in the second, eleven in the third,
eleven in the fourth, and five of the fifth class on the
ground floor, altogether only thirty-five out of eighty-six. A
second auction held the day after Christmas disposed of six
more of the $400 pews and one of the $300, but the
intake still fell far below the sum needed to run the church
and clear it of debt. Here was the first shadow of troubles
to come. At the moment, however, the vestrymen had no
time to worry about finances, for the consecration of the
church was set for the next day.

On December 27, 1816, St. John's day, the vestry and
the wardens met Bishop James Kemp "who proceeded to
the Altar and pronounced the sentence of Consecration.
The Reverend Mr. Norris [of Christ Church in Alexandria]

then read the service and the Reverend William Wilmer delivered an appropriate discourse." It was a solemn occasion, rendered colorful by the blue coats, silver buttons, ruffled shirts, and gleaming shoe buckles of the dignitaries in the congregation and the silks and turbans of their ladies. The December temperatures of a building heated only by four wood or charcoal-burning stoves apparently did not lessen the worshippers' ardor. The talented Benjamin Latrobe composed the dedicatory hymn sung that day:

God of power, God of love,
Earth thy footstool, heaven thy throne,
From the realms of bliss above,
Bow thine ear in mercy down!
Thou who dwell'st in endless space
Fill the house we now prepare
With thy presence and thy grace!
Hear! oh hear thy people's prayer!

Vainly human pow'r essays
Vainly toils the artist's skill
Worthily a shrine to raise
Which Thy Majesty may fill.
But while in thy sacred name
Two or three assembled are
They may Thy sacred promise claim
Thou wilt hear their humble prayer.

Once where o'er this favored land
Savage wilds and darkness spread,
Fostered now by thy kind hand,
Cheerful dwellings rear their head;
Where once frowned the tangled wood,
Fertile fields and meadows smile;
Where the stake of torture stood
Rises now Thy church's pile.

Where the arrow's vengeful flight
Sex, nor age, nor childhood spar'd
Fraud was skill, and pow'r was right,
There thy Gospel's voice is heard!
Heard alas! too oft in vain!
Still with mild prevailing force,
Spreads its love-diffusing reign
Nor shall aught impede its course.

When the hostile firebrand's flash
Reddened late the midnight air,
And the falling cannons crash
Drowned the shrill of wild despair,
Thou, whose nod the storms obey
Midst the wreck of blazing domes
Bad'st him from his fury stay
And respect our private homes.

For these wonders of thy grace
See us bow the grateful knee,
And in this thy holy place,
Consecrate ourselves to thee.
   And when in this Temple's bound
   To thy Altar we repair,
   Breathe thy healing presence round,
   Hear! oh hear thy people's prayer.

The words had special meaning to the congregation gathered at the dedication. If memory of Indian warfare had dimmed, every person present vividly recalled that dreadful night in 1814 when only a torrential rainstorm had checked the conflagration started by "the hostile firebrand's flash." The new "Temple" was truly a thank offering. Thus, alongside Christ Church, St. John's in Georgetown, and Rock Creek Church in the county beyond, St. John's, Washington City, took her place in 1816 as the District of Columbia's fourth Episcopal church.

The pastorate of William Wilmer was brief. In February
the vestry informed him that the Reverend William Hawley
would be "very acceptable" as the "Associate Rector." The
$1,500 annual salary was to be divided equally between the
two clergymen. Penurious as that sum may sound to
modern ears, it equaled that of congressmen at the time.
The lightening of the rector's duties, however, failed to
forestall his resignation in April 1817. He had apparently
made clear in the beginning that his obligations to St.
Paul's in Alexandria and his deep interest in ministerial
education would preclude his keeping his post at St. John's
for any length of time; he was already planning the organization in the District of Columbia of the "Society for the
Education of Pious Young Men for the Ministry of the
Protestant Episcopal Church" which would help to bring
the Virginia Theological Seminary into being in 1823. After
regretfully accepting his resignation, St. John's vestry lost
no time in asking William Hawley to succeed him. The
second rector served the parish for the next twenty-eight
years, through hard times in Washington City, through a
period of doctrinal dispute, and through years of sturdy
growth.

*The Rev. William Hawley, St.
John's Second Rector,
1817-1845.*

William Hawley, a native Vermonter, had read law in
New York City and during the War of 1812 had a short
military career; some of his intimate friends called him
"Captain" long after he had resigned his commission in
order to enter the ministry. A man of lesser learning than
his predecessor and never noted for his oratory, he

preached in simple forcible language, delivering his sermons in a clear loud voice from the wine-glass pulpit. Sixty years after his death, Judge Alexander Hagner recalled the profound impression the rector made upon young members of the congregation. "As he walked from the Chancel through the winding aisles of the old Church to the Vestry Room near the West door in his surplice, and then back again to the Church, attired in the becoming black gown, wearing black kid gloves – one finger of the right hand split to facilitate the turning of leaves of his sermon—with benevolent face and eyes reverently fixed on the brick floor, his appearance, still present to my recollection, seems more impressive in its modest simplicity than that of the high ecclesiastical dignitaries one sees in pompous processions in the splendid Cathedrals in foreign lands." The beautiful black silk gown banded in white and made in London was a present to him from a member of the British Mission in Washington. On the streets of the city to the day of his death in 1845, long after pantaloons, frock coats, and stove-pipe hats had become standard dress, the rector wore short clothes, black silk hose, and a shovel hat.

Strict churchman that he was, he enjoyed the simple pleasures of supping with hospitable parishioners after his pastoral calls and having a game of whist with his hosts. If that pastime appeared unseemly to the Reverend Obadiah Brown of the Baptist Church or to the straight-laced members of the nearby Foundry Methodist Church, most Washingtonians thought it a matter of course in a city where formal "levees," horse-racing, drinking bouts, gossip, and card-playing were virtually the sole diversions, and where many a member of Congress spent most of his evenings around the gambling tables in the hotels. Certainly the rector's casual indulgence in whist evoked no criticism from his own congregation. Throughout his life he maintained a warm friendship with the public-spirited Presbyterian minister, James Laurie, and with the dictatorial but lovable Father William Matthews of Roman Catholic St. Patrick's.

As weddings in those years seldom took place in the church, Mrs. Hawley frequently had to play hostess when her husband married bridal couples at the rectory. Otherwise, except at Sunday services and meetings of the Ladies

Aid, the rector's wife, with a family of children to rear, was seldom in evidence. She attended, to be sure, the wedding at the White House when Mr. Hawley officiated at the marriage of President Monroe's daughter Maria to Samuel Gouverneur. With other mourning Washingtonians, Mrs. Hawley was no doubt present at the funeral services at St. John's for the gallant Commodore Stephen Decatur, killed in a duel shortly after he and his young wife had moved into the handsome house Latrobe had built on the President's Square for the hero of the war with the Barbary pirates. Nevertheless, like several of her 19th century successors, the rector's wife remains a shadowy figure in parish annals.

To the outsider, the handsome stuccoed brick church with its affluent-looking, distinguished congregation of statesmen, military officers, and bankers and their families may have seemed a fortress of religion able to withstand all worldly disasters. Gifts had met nearly half the cost of the land, the building, and furnishings, about $25,000 all told; pew sales and rentals had brought in about $8,500 in subscriptions, and John Tayloe had presented the church with a beautiful Queen Anne silver communion service which he had bought at the auction of the property of the old Lunenburg church in Richmond County, Virginia. But before St. John's was two years old it was confronting financial problems. Some of the purchasers of pews had not yet paid in full, rentals were in arrears, and current expenses, including the rector's and the sexton's salaries, were outrunning income. Although the United States was enjoying a period of booming prosperity during this post-war "Era of Good Feeling," few Washingtonians were wealthy. Speculation, moreover, caught the most respectable and generally conservative citizens in its toils. The vestry of St. John's, in attempts to meet its obligations, optimistically tried various devices — the appointment of a collector of rents, higher purchase prices for pews, special assessments, and an auction of unsold pews which bidders might buy on six to twelve months' credit "for negotiable notes with good endorsers."

Despite the difficulties of raising cash from pewholders, a proposal to enlarge the church, install additional pews, and thus hopefully increase revenue, found some favor. Mr. Hawley was to approach the new architect of the Capitol, Charles Bulfinch of Boston, for a plan and an estimate of the cost of extending the church; if Mr. Bulfinch's ideas seemed impractical, an alternative would be to use the drawings Latrobe had prepared before he left Washington in 1817. Some of the vestrymen plainly considered such procedures unwise. Dr. Blake and Roger Weightman resigned.

The vestry, elected on Easter Monday 1818, clung to the scheme of enlarging the church. General Swift and James Hoban, architect of the original White House, examined the church building and reported that Bulfinch's plan could be carried out "with the most perfect safety." Subscriptions to shares should cover the costs. But, tacitly acknowledging possible trouble in securing subscriptions, the vestry voted to wait till the money was on hand before going further. And, as the cautious had feared, subscriptions came in discouragingly slowly. In order to stretch current income the pews still unpaid for had to be resold, while appeals for help went out to sister churches in Philadelphia, New York, Boston, and Baltimore. A more ominous decision was to pay the rector's salary at the end of every three months; if the church then had insufficient funds, the treasurer was to borrow from the banks on what would appear to be the church's distinctly shaky credit. Late in 1818, the nationwide orgy of speculation collapsed, reducing high priced assets to a fraction of their inflated value and leaving supposedly well-to-do men on the verge of bankruptcy.

St. John's treasurer, Thomas Gillis, resigned in February 1819. The following Sunday Mr. Hawley's sermon took the form of a plea to the congregation to rescue the church. The collection on the first Sunday in every month thereafter was allotted to reducing the church debt. Yet, manifestly convinced that the Lord would care for His own, the vestry chose to spend the collection of Communion Sunday for the purchase of two silver plates. Otherwise every conceivable means of raising money and reducing expenditures went into effect. A measure of the financial pressure lay in the decision to lease the lot adjoining the church to Archibald McPhail for a school, a transaction that netted the parish $15 a year in ground rent. The Bank of the

Metropolis at this juncture agreed to fund the church debt of $5,053. By October every collection was assigned to meeting the interest on the debt, every pewholder received a formal letter setting forth St. John's financial plight, while the vestry notified delinquent pew renters that suits for nonpayment would soon be filed against them. Still the acute discomfort of attending services in bitter weather in a building heated only by four stoves forced the vestry to consider installing three additional stoves. And as fire was an ever-present hazard in a community whose fire-fighting equipment consisted of householders' leather buckets and an engine and hose in every ward (but with only the wells in the public squares to supply water to the hose), the vestry felt impelled to take out a $6,000 fire insurance policy.

Although the effects of the panic lasted longer in Washington than in the commercial centers of the country, the federal city benefitted from the stability of the federal payroll: every month the Treasury paid out to every government employee one to twelve double gold eagles, depending on whether he were a laborer, a clerk, or a cabinet officer. As the congregation of St. John's included a considerable proportion of high-ranking officials, by midsummer of 1820 the vestry decided to risk an investment of $3,500 in adding three stoves and enlarging the church according to Benjamin Latrobe's plan. Extending the west transept toward 16th Street and thus changing the Greek to a Latin cross would provide space for fifty more pews; if sold for $100 apiece those would more than meet the estimated cost. The addition of a Doric-columned Roman porch and three doors from it opening into the vestibule to the church would help to preserve the balanced proportions of the original building. So, under the direction of Colonel George Bomford, chief of the Army Ordnance Department, the alterations began which would transform the exterior of the church essentially into the structure we see today.

The pillared porch and three doors now placed the main entrance on the west. Inside the church, the gallery, from the first a distinctive feature of Latrobe's design, covered the entire westward extension. Stairs went up to it from a corner of the vestibule. Although Latrobe apparently had not included drawings for a steeple, a graceful bell tower was an important addition. No record tells who designed it. Its completion had to wait upon subscriptions, but in July 1822 the slender three-stage rectangular tower topped by a gilded, thimble-shaped cap rose to its full forty-foot height above the columned porch. From a British cannon captured during the war and then presented to St. John's by President Monroe, the Paul Revere works of Boston cast the thousand-pound bronze bell placed in the steeple. Until then, St. Patrick's Roman Catholic Church had had the only bell in the city. Some Washingtonians reportedly objected to the "incongruity" of a rectangular belfry for a church built on classical lines, but everyone within earshot delighted in the sweet tones of the bell. It rang out not only to summon people to Sunday worship and to mark days of public thanksgiving, but also to toll at the death of a President and to sound fire alarms for the city. As the bell rope hung down into the vestibule where it somewhat obstructed the center door, in 1824 flooring was laid in the steeple with access to it from the gallery. Unwilling to superimpose extraneous adornment on the church's chaste

St. John's Church after 1822 Renovation.

interior, the vestry declined the offer of a large painting of
St. Simeon's Prophecy which the would-be donor wanted
to hang in a conspicuous place. The enlargement of the
church did not, however, provide space for a Sunday
School. Consequently, in 1828, the vestry rented a room in
a nearby building where William James presided as super-
intendent over several generations of pupils.

For the next fourteen years further architectural changes
were kept to a minimum. In 1830 the moving of the vestry
room to the south west corner of the vestibule contrived
space for two new pews behind the altar. Six years later
the permanent closing of the H Street entrance made room
for another two. But a large window cut through the south
wall over them necessitated shifting the organ to the north
transept. That arrangement soon proved unsatisfactory.
Ever since the vestry had decided in 1834 to engage a
salaried choir, music had become an all-important part of
the service; experience quickly pointed to the desirability
of seating the choir near the organ. In 1839, therefore,
when the vestry purchased a larger organ, choir and organ
were relocated in the west gallery.

Meanwhile, although the founding of the now extinct
Trinity Parish in 1827 had cut off a sizable piece of St.
John's original parish, by 1840 the growth of Washington
to a city of some 16,800 white inhabitants, 4,800 free
Negroes, and 1,700 slaves swelled attendance at St. John's.
Free Negroes, to be sure, rarely crowded in upon "the
Quality," but slave-owning parishioners who wanted their
bondsmen to attend services had to find places for them.
Visitors to the capital often added to the congregation. By
the autumn of 1842 more seating capacity had become
imperative.

The committee put in charge of finding a solution to the
problem hit upon a relatively simple scheme: replacement
of the roomy box pews with narrow, low-backed, long
pews set closely one behind the other. If long-legged occupants felt cramped, every pew-owner welcomed an accompanying innovation. Wooden flooring, laid over the old
brick with a foot of space between, furnished insulation
from the icy drafts of midwinter. Presumably because the
raised floor robbed the columns of height, less massive

pillars replaced the old. The remodelling changed the appearance of the church's interior, but the committee could point out that knocking out the walls, the only alternative way to gain floor space, would have destroyed completely the exquisite proportions of Latrobe's original design. Two novel features reflected merely a change of taste. Grisaille painting of the chancel with tromp d'oeil framed in molding marked a departure from the unembellished simplicity characterizing Latrobe's treatment. Outside blinds at the windows were a second deviation from the original style of the building. Later generations came to be grateful that the alterations were not of a structural nature and, therefore, not irredeemable.

One distinct loss, however, was the substitution of a conventional pulpit for the graceful wine glass pulpit with its charming light spiral of steps by which the preacher mounted to an elevation commanding his audience. Wheels attached to the tripodal base had fitted into iron tracks laid in the floor and thus permitted shifting the pulpit from the front of the chancel toward the center of the church. As Bishop Ravenscroft later told the story, on one occasion when he was preaching under the dome, "the pulpit ran away with me. It had been wheeled out of its place and fastened with a snap catch. I was conscious of the distinguished and notable audience before me, and was preaching to them with vigorous earnestness, when of a sudden I felt the pulpit beneath me to be gliding away. Faster and faster towards the side wall of the church it was moving, and gaining rapidly as it went. The congregation were agitated; I was helpless; and I assure you I was considerably out of countenance when we stopped suddenly, and with a bump at the end of our notable journey." With the new stationary pulpit a similar hejira never recurred.

St. John's followed low rather than high church ritual in these years before the Oxford Movement caused a tumult within the Protestant Episcopal world. Secretary of State John Quincy Adams, self-styled "Independent Congregationalist," nevertheless privately believed that the rector interpreted Christianity with excessive rigidity. "Mr. Sparks, the Unitarian, preached for the first time at the Capitol to a crowded auditory," ran an entry of December 1821 in

Adams' diary. "His election as Chaplain of the House of
Representatives occasioned much surprise and has been followed by unusual symptoms of intolerance. Mr. Hawley,
the Episcopal preacher at St. John's Church, last Sunday
preached a sermon of coarse invective upon the House,
who, he said, by this act has voted Christ out-of-doors, and
he enjoined all the people of his flock NOT to set their
feet within the Capitol to hear Mr. Sparks." A day or two
later a New York congressman introduced a motion to
cancel the appointment of the man who would later become President of Harvard College. That "extraordinary
mode of opposition," Adams observed, "has only served to
render Sparks more conspicuous and to sharpen the curios-
ity to hear him." The deeply religious but open-minded
New Englander also objected to "the vehement and terrify-
ing tones of oratory" in which many Episcopalian pastors
of the day, especially those trained at Princeton, were
indulging. "They have been driven to this recourse by the
desertion of their following. Fear and Hope are the two
balances on which all religious faith is built. But fear is . . .
always a more [powerful] agent than Hope." Although Mr.
Hawley usually eschewed the fire and brimstone theme,
Adams, finding the rector's sermons lacking in depth, ordinarily attended some other church on Sunday mornings but
from time to time went to Sunday evening prayers at St.
John's. Mrs. Adams and the children regularly attended
there. The Bishop of Maryland, on the other hand, was
critical of Mr. Hawley for reasons very different from those
of John Quincy Adams.

To the Protestant churchman of the 1970's the doctrinal
controversy that developed at St. John's in 1825 may
seem to verge on the petty. The closely written pages of
the vestry minutes bear witness, however, to the importance the men of the time attached to the questions involved. A protest from vestryman Major Charles J. Nourse
launched the debate when he complained indignantly about

a declaration the rector had made the preceeding Sunday
before administering communion: "In addition to the members of this Church, I invite all Christians of other denominations who are in good standing in their respective
societies to remain and participate in this Holy Ordinance,

but to such as *refuse this offer let them recollect in leaving this house* that by so *doing* they have this *day denied* the Lord Jesus *Christ before men* and that he will *deny them hereafter* before his *Father in Heaven.*" Mr. Hawley's "anathematizing of non-communicants," Major Nourse contended, was in every way "unauthorized . . . and highly offensive." The major himself had not taken communion that Sunday. He begged the vestry to take a stand against "a principle so full of intolerance." When the rest of the vestry, after much soul-searching and study, decreed the rector's pronouncement in keeping with the Scriptures, the outraged Major presented the case to the Bishop. Waving aside Major Nourse's request for vindication, the Bishop addressed himself to Mr. Hawley's aberration in suggesting that members of other denominations might partake of the sacrament at St. John's.

Only the year before, Bishop Kemp had visited the parish, summoned the vestry and the wardens to an inquiry into their stewardship, and investigated the spiritual condition of the congregation. Any dissatisfaction he may have felt at his findings was now obviously heightened. "It has been a source of great grief to me," he wrote, "that in Washington, the Capital of this vast and enlightened Nation, the resort of strangers from all quarters and of foreigners from all nations, the services of the Church should not be performed in a Style Suited to her Character, and in Conformity to her usages and Rubricks." To invite members of other religious bodies to share in the sacrament of the Eucharist was an impropriety "in which some of our Clergy seem to indulge", but it was "altogether at variance with the Twelfth Canon of Maryland . . . The minister shall satisfy himself that Holy Communion goes only to registered communicants of his own or other Protestant Episcopal Churches."

However discomfitted by that reprimand, neither the rector nor the vestry pursued the matter further. Major Nourse withdrew. But scarcely had the doctrinal contretemps subsided that secular problems, namely money, overwhelmed church officials. In 1827 they adopted the expedient of paying Mr. Hawley only $1,156 of his $1,500 salary. Indeed, contrary to later belief that St. John's from the first was a wealthy parish, during most of its first thirty years debts hung like an albatross around the neck of each vestry in turn. Expectations that pew sales and rentals would meet all expenses once the church was enlarged proved ill-founded. Washington in the 1820's and 1830's was a poor city. Due chiefly to overly optimistic investment in Chesapeake and Ohio Canal stock, the city corporation itself faced bankruptcy in 1833 and was only rescued by congressional intervention. For twelve years Mr. Hawley acquiesced in "temporary" cuts in salary, because, a vestryman later averred, reduction of the sums owed the bank was "the one means of saving the Church from the auctioneer's hammer." Not until 1839, following upon a note of "asperity" from the rector, did the vestry assure him of regular payment of his full stipend.

Otherwise, relations between Mr. Hawley and his congregation were peaceful. When a feud split Washington society over according civilities to the wife of Andrew Jackson's Secretary of War, a number of St. John's parishioners led by Mrs. John Calhoun, wife of the Vice President, defied the President's mandate to receive the notorious Peggy Eaton whom they considered an immoral female. Mr. Hawley kept out of the ensuing battles, but the young minister of the Second Presbyterian Church felt obliged to announce his disapproval of the President's protege. The upshot was a summons to the White House, a stinging rebuke for maligning a pure and innocent woman, and the loss of Andrew Jackson as member of the minister's congregation. Thenceforward Old Hickory generally attended St. John's. In 1836 when the recently widowed Dolley Madison returned to Washington to take up residence on Lafayette Square, she asked to be confirmed and became a communicant of St. John's.

An aura of serenity enveloped the parish during the next decade. But if the congregation was at peace with itself and heaven and earth, in John Quincy Adams' opinion only worldliness and an ignoring of moral questions made that possible. "Old Man Eloquent," who spent the last sixteen years of his life as a member of the House of Representatives in fighting for free speech and freedom of petition against slavery, did not publicly voice his views on religion or single out St. John's for reprobation, but he obviously felt that a congregation which included so many influential public figures was shirking its moral responsibilities. "There were scarcely thirty persons in the house," he noted in his diary in 1838 upon his return from an evening service at St. John's. "The neglect of public worship in this city is an increasing evil. . . The counterfeit character of a very large portion of the Christian ministry in this country is disclosed in the dissertions growing up in all the Protestant churches on the subject of slavery. The abolitionists assume as the first principle of all their movements that slavery is SIN. The opponents, halting between the alternative of denying directly this position and of admitting the duty binding upon them to bear testimony against it, are prevaricating with their own consciences, and taking their learning and ingenuity to prove that the Bible sanctions slavery. . . This question of slavery is convulsing the Congregational Churches in Massachusetts, it is deeply agitating the Methodists, it had already completed a Schism in the Presbyterian Church, two separate bodies of which are now in session in Philadelphia." No church in the national capital was as yet willing to face the issue. The congregation at St. John's, heavily weighted as it was with southerners and high-ranking government officials, preferred to think the peculiar institution no affair for the church to meddle in. When Mr. Hawley baptized and married parishioners' slaves, their masters were at pains to explain to their bondsmen that the ceremony had not endowed them with freedom in this world.

"The fraility of human, all human enjoyments, and the awful vicissitudes woven into the lot of mortal man" was brought home to Washingtonians by the death of President William Henry Harrison on Palm Sunday in 1841. Only the Sunday before, the courtly old Virginian had stood at the doors of St. John's after the morning service greeting his friends and gallantly escorting ladies to their carriages; he had worn no overcoat in the chilly wind but, as a courtesy to an American glove-making firm, had donned white silk gloves which had on the back "in brown and gayest green, a replica of the famous Log Cabin," his campaign emblem. Now he lay dead, a victim of pneumonia. Mr. Hawley,

perplexed about how to conduct the services for this the
first President to die in office, sought the advice of John
Quincy Adams. Mr. Adams' memoirs record the request. He
assured Mr. Hawley of the propriety of reading the prayer
for the President of the United States as the Prayer Book
gave it, although, the former President added, "a variation
of expression" might be suitable. "With proper religious
solemnity and with the simplicity congenial to our repub-
lican institutions," three days later the rector read the
funeral service in the East Room of the White House.
Standing by the coffin with its black velvet pall, he told
"the assembled auditory" that General Harrison "had expressed his regret at not having joined in full communion
with the church, and that it was his intention to have done
so on the ensuing Easter Day—next Sunday."

Slightly less than four years later, in January 1845,
funeral services were held at St. John's for William Hawley.
As he had requested, the Reverend Dr. Stephen H. Tyng of
Philadelphia preached the funeral sermon. Interment was
alongside the chancel against the north wall of the church
in which the rector had served a longer pastorate than any
successor was to have. The next Sunday the Reverend
Smith Pyne, who had become Assistant Minister in 1844,
conducted a memorial service, while at the Presbyterian
Church James Laurie spoke feelingly of his old friend. The
vestry passed resolutions of gratitude to the man who had
given most of his life to St. John's. The congregation later
placed in the church a tablet inscribed in his memory:
"Blessed are the poor in heart, for they shall see God." So
the first era of St. John's closed quietly.

2

Years Of Turmoil

The second generation of St. John's Parish was to know troubles of a kind its founders had escaped. For several years after the Reverend Smith Pyne accepted the rectorship in March 1845, it is true, the church was able to enjoy peace of mind and spirit. The new minister was a man of exceptional cultivation. The Ireland-born son of "people of fortune" who had moved when he was a small child to Charleston, South Carolina, Smith Pyne had grown up in that southern capital, toured Europe with a tutor, and completed his formal education at Oxford. He had then filled a post in New York City where John H. Spencer, President Tyler's Secretary of War, had observed his work. Spencer had prevailed upon St. John's vestry to call him to Washington. There his fine mind, his literary attainments, and his brilliant conversation immediately won him a place in the most agreeable circle of society. His contemporaries likened him to Sir Philip Sidney. In the pulpit his beautiful enunciation and his perception of the pathos of passages in the Bible made his rendition of the Scriptures a memorable experience for his listeners.

The congregation grew steadily, although death thinned the ranks of the original members, and the forming of three new parishes, Epiphany, Ascension and St. Andrew's, reduced the geographical reach of St. John's. At the Church of the Presidents, sons and daughters of its founders carried

25

on, some of them purchasing two adjoining pews in order
to accommodate three generations of families for each of
whom one of the roomy old box pews had once sufficed.
Names already or soon-to-be famous in American history
continued to appear in the parish records—General Winfield
Scott, Secretary of State Lewis Cass, Secretary of the Navy
and historian George Bancroft, Senators John Forsyth,
John Y. Mason, Salmon P. Chase, Hamilton Fish, and
William Seward, to name but a few. Most of the British
ministers to the United States also attended with some
regularity. When the President came, visitors filled every
available seat.

*The Rev. Smith Pyne, Third
Rector, 1845-1864.*

Financially the church prospered. The indebtedness,
some $9,000 in 1845, dropped to $4,000 in 1850, despite
the expense of reroofing the building and enclosing the
grounds with a picket fence. An exchange of property,
located in another part of the city, for a lot at 16th and I
Streets meanwhile extended church holdings in the vicinity
of Lafayette Square. Shortly after the extinction of the
church debt in 1853, the vestry raised the rector's salary
from $2,000 to $2,500, engaged an assistant minister, voted
to set aside some $420 a year for music, and pledged the
Sunday collections to the support of the parish school
which the ladies' Benevolent Society had started in 1851.
Plans to build a chapel in the western part of the city
began to take shape while negotiations were under way to
acquire a new burial ground to replace the parish cemetery

acquired in 1820 in the then thinly peopled section of Washington known as the "Northern Liberties." An agreement entered into with Rock Creek Church releasing part of the cemetery there to St. John's led in 1860 to the removal of the coffins interned in the old St. John's burial ground. Meantime the newly organized Gentlemen's Charitable Association founded a Church Home for needy elderly members of the parish. Inmates and matron occupied a rented house on H Street until, in 1859, all the Episcopal churches in the city joined in establishing a single home for their impoverished aged.

Material well-being and every-increasing prestige, however, could not obliterate the mounting uneasiness pervading St. John's and the city in the 1850's. When the treaty ending the war with Mexico added a large slice of the continent to the United States, the extension of slavery into the newly acquired territories had become a burning issue throughout the country. "The slavery question," a young Washingtonian had written apprehensively in the summer of 1848, "is here the all-absorbing topic of the day." By 1850 most permanent residents of Washington, including presumably slave-owners among St. John's parishioners, had shed objections to seeing emancipation take effect in the District of Columbia, but by no means all of them were ready to have the federal government interfere with the property rights of citizens of the states. In the midst of the heated debates in Congress, the death of President Zachary Taylor in July 1850 heightened Washington's uncertainties. Dr. Pyne conducted the solemn funeral services, but, the day after the old general had been laid to rest, the battle on Capitol Hill resumed. The compromise acts passed that autumn seemed for a year or two to promise "peace in our time," and, to the gratification of the local community, rid the District of the slave trade. But by 1854 tensions between North and South had reached a new pitch. Every thoughtful person in the capital was aware of the painful possibility of a truly "irrepressible conflict." Churchmen could no longer wholly ignore the moral questions involved in the perpetuation of slavery.

For the first time in St. John's history a complete turnover in the vestry occurred in the spring of 1854. No

mention of slavery nor indeed any explanation for the
sudden change found its way into the church records, but
the timing of the upheaval is suggestive of deep-seated
differences over what constituted Christian duty. As the
decade wore on, members of the congregation, such as
Senator William Seward, Senator Salmon P. Chase, Captain
Peter Hagner, Francis and Montgomery Blair, could not be
expected to see eye to eye with parishioners who, like
General Joseph E. Johnston, defended the slavocracy and
states' rights. President James Buchanan, another communicant at the Church of the Presidents, vainly attempted
to steer a middle course in public policy, but sentiment in
every church in the city was divided. With the exception of
the young Unitarian minister who spoke out from the
pulpit in strong denunciation of slavery and lost his pastorate for so doing, all ministers in Washington sedulously
avoided open discussion on the explosive subject.

If Dr. Pyne's early ties with Charleston, South Carolina,
led some of his congregation to suppose that he would
betray sympathy with the South, they proved mistaken. On

View of Lafayette Park and St. John's Church, circa 1860.

an anxious Sunday morning eight days before the inauguration of Abraham Lincoln, Senator Seward accompanied by a tall gaunt man "in plain black clothes, with black whiskers, and hair well trimmed" occupied Pew #1 at St. John's. Nobody recognized the stranger. Dr. Pyne preached on a text from I Corinthians 7:31, "And they that use this world, as not abusing it: for the fashion of this world passeth away," a theme that permitted allusions to the perilous state of the nation and the impending change in administration. Not until the service was over and Senator Seward introduced his guest did the rector and congregation learn that the President-elect had been listening attentively to the sermon.

When South Carolinian hotheads fired on the American flag flying over Fort Sumter in Charleston harbor and plunged the divided nation into war, most members of St. John's, already coming to be known locally as the "Church of the Army and Navy," loyally supported the Union. The roster of parishioners who served their country with distinction during the Civil War is impressive. Because floor space

View of Chancel, St. John's Church, 1860's.

was limited, the church, unlike many others in Washington, was not converted into a hospital. The parish school and the Episcopal Church Home closed down, but services at the church continued without interruption until late 1864; seats unoccupied by owners at the battle fronts were filled Sunday after Sunday by newcomers to the war-swollen capital. A story that had gone the rounds soon after President Lincoln's inauguration was still applicable. The tale told of a highly recommended young office seeker whom the President had felt obliged to reject but in such kindly fashion that the young man had suggested leaving his papers at the White House. "Don't do it!" exclaimed Lincoln. "Keep 'em. They might—now mind you I don't say they will, but they might—gain you a membership at St. John's."

"A Christian without a creed," never a member of any church, Lincoln himself did not seek that privilege. But his relations with the rector and members of St. John's were cordial. When the rector began to hold daily afternoon prayer services, legend has it that the troubled President often slid unobtrusively into a back pew during that half hour. Dr. Pyne felt free to intercede with him on behalf of a parishioner, the stormy Admiral Charles Wilkes. The Admiral had been court-martialled for insubordination and consigned to three years' suspension. Dr. Pyne, in begging the President to reduce the sentence to a sharp censure, concluded by speaking of "the amount of obligation and attachment by which I have long felt myself bound to you both in your official and personal character." The President cut the Admiral's enforced retirement to a year.

A reminiscence of March 1862 recounted by the wife of Admiral John Rodgers gives a picture of the anxieties of those years. Word had reached Washington on a Saturday afternoon that the heavily plated Confederate ship *Merrimack* had steamed down the river from Richmond. With only the frigate *Congress* and a sloop to intercept the iron-clad, disaster for the Union looked imminent. On Sunday morning members of St. John's congregation stood outside the church telling each other apprehensively what the powerful *Merrimack* might destroy. "The Church bell brought the people in at the last minute. In the middle of Mr. Pyne's sermon the sexton came down the aisle, touched Mr. Fox, the Assistant Secretary of the Navy, and whispered something." Mr. Fox hastily went out. "Then the sexton came down the other aisle of the church and bent over the General in command of the defense of Washington and he departed at once. The sexton came again and took out old Commodore Smith whose son was captain of the *Congress*. When he was told that the *Congress* had surrendered, he said, 'The *Congress* surrendered! — then my Joe is dead!' Then General Meigs went out, and then Mr. Pyne clapped his sermon book together and gave the benediction, and the congregation came out in fear and trembling, wondering when they would see the *Merrimack* coming up the Potomac River to bombard the White House and the rest of Washington. But the very next day the little

Monitor, a new type of ship, appeared at Hampton Roads and injured the *Merrimack* so severely that she went back to Richmond and never did anything any more."

Dr. Pyne's sermons repeatedly brought comfort to his listeners. Passionate Unionist though he was, he spoke less of victories "in this unnatural contest" than of the "bright omen of the future", the instinctive sympathies persisting between friend and foe, which would in time bring about reconciliation. Events after the fall of Vicksburg supplied him with a telling illustration: "A beseiged fortress, bravely defended, yielded, and, forthwith, the men in late hostile array and deadly conflict were hand in hand and arm in arm. My brethren, there is no moral gulf fixed on this side of eternity."

For obscure reasons, a falling out between rector and vestry occurred in the summer of 1864. Dr. Pyne, overworked and in ill health, instructed the vestrymen to hold meetings only at his call. The indignant vestry wrote to the Bishop but, getting no guidance from that quarter, continued to hold meetings from which the rector absented himself. At these "irregular" sessions the vestry sold some of the land near the church on 16th Street for $800, approved the church ladies' project of acquiring a new organ, and closed the church down from August till October, 1864, in order to make alterations. On November 1st Dr. Pyne submitted his resignation. The vestry promptly accepted it without comment. The abrupt departure of the ordinarily urbane Dr. Pyne left the parish floundering. He volunteered to conduct services during the winter and the spring of 1865 until the church could engage a new rector, but the vestry stiffly rejected his offer. The new organ, specially built by a firm in Massachusetts and purchased with money advanced by Dr. R. A. Lacey of the vestry, sounded out for months to a congregation over which a succession of temporary ministers presided on Sundays.

On April 20th, 1865 Dr. Lacey as president of the vestry signed a resolution: "That the distinguishing characteristics of Abraham Lincoln—his undeviating integrity and truthfulness, his gentle and forgiving disposition, his kindness and sympathy with the suffering and oppressed, his uniform recognition of an overruling Providence in all national affairs, his wise statesmanship, harmonizing differences of patriotic opinion, and always tempering justice with mercy—will enshrine him in the hearts of his countrymen forever, and that the purity of his life will shine brighter when contrasted with the infamy of the deed that terminated it." St. John's was draped in black for six months, and every member of the vestry wore an armband of mourning during that period. Only the final capitulation of the Confederacy and the return home of men who had been serving in the Army and Navy during the four bitter years of war restored peace of heart to the parish. When the Reverend John Vaughan Lewis of Norwich, Connecticut, accepted the rectorship to take effect on September 1, 1865, St. John's looked forward to an unbroken era of usefulness. No one foresaw that internal dissension would soon develop within the parish or that tribulations almost as acute as those of war-time would long afflict the entire city.

No matter what the Reverend Dr. Lewis had heard about post-war Washington while he was living in the small, homogeneous town of Norwich, he must have been shocked upon his arrival in the capital in the autumn of 1865. Poverty blanketed whole sections of the city, particularly neighborhoods into which Negro immigrants from the rural South continued to pour, turning the District of Columbia, so the saying ran, into "the poorhouse of Virginia." Neglected, friendless children, white and black alike, roamed the streets in numbers far in excess of what the Washington City Orphan Asylum, the two Roman Catholic orphanages, and the Newsboys' Aid Society could care for. The Freedmen's Bureau, established in March, was trying to find housing and work for indigent Negroes, and the national and local Freedmen's Relief associations were carrying on their activities of material aid and teaching the newcomers how to help themselves, but termination of war-time jobs and the consequent spread of unemployment constantly broadened the dimensions of community problems. Hospital service was meagre. The plight of impoverished old people of both races was little short of desperate. Every eleemosynary and religious body in the city faced overwhelming tasks. The Episcopal clergy, believing their first obligation to be the nurturing of spiritual life in the community, in December 1865 formed the Washington Convocation "to erect new parishes by collecting and organizing congregations in destitute localities and encouraging the building of new Churches." The words of the statement of purpose were Dr. Lewis', the first secretary of the Convocation.

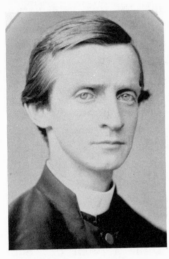

The Rev. John Vaughn Lewis,
Fourth Rector, 1865-1880.

   Unlike the gentle Mr. Hawley and the brilliant, intellectually stimulating Smith Pyne, John Vaughan Lewis was an organizer. The piercing-eyed, thin-lipped, ascetic face shown in a yellowing old photograph portrays a person not to be turned aside from his duty as he saw it. Besides ministering to his flock at St. John's, he early revealed two additional objectives: a large-scale program of parish charities and enlargement of the church edifice in order to attract and accommodate a bigger congregation. Unfortunately, in pursuing these goals, he frequently exhibited more zeal than tact or patience. When the vestry did not see eye to eye with him, usually over money matters, but sometimes over how far the authority of each extended, quarrels divided the parish. Yet during the troubled fifteen years of his pastorate, St. John's broadened its outlook and undertook good works of considerable magnitude.
   Initially Dr. Lewis apparently assumed that here was a wealthy parish needing only a strong hand at the helm.

"You will permit me to say," his letter accepting the post had run, "that the rector of such a Parish ought not to be subjected to any anxieties concerning his support and to record my conviction that the Parish ought, for its sake and mine, to take immediate steps to secure a suitable parsonage which, with the salary named by you [$3,000], would seem to be a comfortable provision for my temporal wants." The vestry complied with his request by leasing and refurbishing for him and his wife a house at 19th and I Streets at an annual rental of $600. But the recent purchase of a new organ, a commitment of $1,000 a year for salaries for organist and choir, the decision to install gas lights around the dome of the church, and the necessity of making extensive repairs, including the reroofing of the building, led the holders of the purse strings to exercise caution about further expenditures. The rector had other ideas. Money he believed could always be found for a worthy cause.

After his installation, Dr. Lewis' first proposal was to found a girls' school for which, he asserted, the parish should raise a $20,000 endowment. St. John's Hall, as he outlined the scheme, was to ensure a solid religious as well as a secular education for little girls between the ages of 6 and 14. As $8 to $10 tuition for a ten-week term might be too high for many Washington families, he asked that a scholarship fund be placed at his disposal which he could dispense secretly. Whatever their dismay at the figures he spoke of and their doubts about the overriding importance of the project, the vestrymen voiced no objection to the rector's issuing a prospectus and soliciting subscriptions; after all, the diocesan Convention was urging the establishment of church schools everywhere. So, in the spring of 1866, St. John's Hall opened in a building on I Street near the house once occupied by Secretary of State James Monroe.

On December 27, 1866, St. John's celebrated the semicentennial of the consecration of the church. Nonogenarian Roger Weightman, the only surviving member of the first vestry, was present. Seven ministers from Washington City, New York, and the Naval Academy took part, a "double antiphonal choir" sang the chants, and Dr. Lewis delivered an "Historical Sketch of the Parish" in which he listed the parish institutions: St. John's Hall, St. John's Guild for young men, the Scholarship Fund, and St. John's Home and Mission House. Of those four, neither the school nor the Guild fell into the category of charities as such, and the Scholarship Fund represented a long-time interest, carrying on the work which Dr. Wilmer had inaugurated in 1817 through his Society for Education of Pious Young Men for the Ministry of the Protestant Episcopal Church. The Home and Mission House, on the contrary, was a new departure.

St. John's Hall early became self-supporting. When Dr. Lewis' first assistant minister took charge of it in the fall of 1867, he proudly described it as a "French and English Boarding and Day Seminary" with forty pupils enrolled and four instructors besides himself. Its stability thus ensured, it ceased after 1868 to maintain an intimate tie to St. John's. Well before then, the Home and Mission House and a chapel for colored Episcopalians sponsored by the Washington Convocation were preoccupying the attention of charitable-minded parishioners of St. John's. The Home, at first located on K Street at Connecticut Avenue, was a missionary undertaking "for the poor of the First Ward, irrespective of denomination or color." It differed consequently from the chapel and every similar enterprise the parish had ever attempted. In launching St. Mary's Chapel, the rector of Epiphany Church had been the moving spirit. During 1865 he had conducted "cottage meetings" for his Negro parishioners and interested them and their friends in forming a separate congregation in the predominantly Negro neighborhood of Foggy Bottom. When he induced Secretary of War Stanton early in 1867 to let them move a chapel originally built for soldiers at Kalorama Hospital to a site on 23rd Street near G, and Dr. Lewis persuaded a well-to-do member of St. John's to donate a plot of land there, St. Mary's Chapel became a reality. For the next six years gifts from the Convocation helped support it, while a young deacon, an assistant to Dr. Lewis, conducted the religious services there. The Home and Mission House had a more complex history.

As a bi-racial charity with no sectarian strings attached, the Home depended in part on contributions from the

entire community, but St. John's parishioners, urged on by
Dr. Lewis, made themselves responsible for it. In November
1866 the vestry declared itself the "corporation" and
appointed a board of managers consisting of six men and
twelve women. The vestry was to disburse the money
subscribed for the work and add from time to time such
funds as the church treasury could spare; the managers
were to supervise the program, pay the bills, and submit a
formal report to the vestry on All Soul's Day every year.
Gifts of land which the vestry sold met most of the initial
costs of renting headquarters and running the Home. In
1868 two members of St. John's vestry approached General
O. O. Howard, head of the federal Freedmen's Bureau, and
obtained from him a pledge of $100 a month "in aid of
charities and for purchases for the Home, and when called
upon, would give the regular portion of dessicated vegetables." The vegetables, probably grown at the Freedmen's
Village farm on General Lee's former estate in Arlington,
indicated that the Home distributed food to needy colored
people. Nothing in the parish or diocesan Convention
records suggests that the Home supplied living quarters for
its beneficiaries. When young John M. E. McKee became its
"agent" at the end of 1868 he spoke of "his labors in this
field of usefulness ... [as] cherished privileges," but he
failed to spell out the exact nature of those labors.

Whatever the services of the mission, they soon became
too expensive for St. John's vestry to endorse. Two years
after the project got underway, the vestry announced that
it could no longer be the corporation; it would handle the
real estate of the Home, but the board of managers would
have to raise the money to run it. Indignantly the rector
inscribed on the margin of the vestry minutes: "Illegal!" It
was at this point that he assigned his assistant, Mr. McKee,
to the task of acting as agent. The earnest young agent
informed the diocesan Convention that the rector's "hearty
support.... and the practical sympathy and cordial cooperation he [McKee] has realized from liberal-souled
parishioners of St. John's" kept the Home in operation, but
obviously on a hand to mouth basis. In the spring of 1869
a gift of land at E and 21st Streets donated by a parishioner for "the Home and Parish School" promised to

permit the erection of "a suitable temporary building." The vestry exchanged the lot for one on 16th Street near the church, and there in a small house the Home carried on its work until 1876.

While Dr. Lewis succeeded in preserving the mission, his relations with his vestry rapidly worsened. His dissatisfaction with the performance of the choir sparked one angry quarrel, but that controversy paled before the fight over enlarging the church. The Junior Warden, Charles Gordon, had first presented a proposal in 1866 which the vestry shelved; a year later General Montgomery Meigs offered another plan, one of his own design, and gave a $100 government bond to start a building fund. The rector consulted a New York architect who assured him that, by knocking out all the original walls of the church, seating capacity could be doubled at a cost of probably not much more than $20,000. Again the vestry postponed action, for a majority was dubious about the scheme. Some of the members, furthermore, were apparently wondering about the consequences of losing another segment of the parish. In 1866, when a recently started mission in the "west end" had asked to be set off from St. John's, the vestry had been loath to agree, but in 1867 reluctantly sanctioned the division. The erection of St. Paul's not only stripped the parent parish of a sizable, albeit not yet wealthy, domain, but, upon completion of St. Paul's Church early the next year, seemed likely to reduce the size of the congregation at Lafayette Square. While in some people's eyes those facts justified doing nothing to St. John's, in the opinion of Dr. Lewis and other parishioners, the best way to maintain the position of the Church of the Presidents — especially now that neither President Andrew Johnson nor President-elect U. S. Grant showed any inclination to attend — was to follow the course adopted in 1820: enlarge the church, install more pews, and count on sales and rentals to expand parish resources. The rector at last inveigled wardens and vestry into letting him obtain new plans calculated to show the feasibility of his ideas. He presented the results in March 1869. The vestry acquiesced in starting immediate negotiations with contractors.

Whether opposition sprang principally from aesthetic considerations, from sentimental attachment to the old building, or from sheer anxiety about the cost and belief that the money might better be spent on charitable projects, the response was not what proponents of the plan expected. A month after the vestry's acceptance of the rector's cherished plan, new officials elected by qualified voters at the annual parish meeting rescinded their predecessors' decision. Dr. Lewis was furious. Unable to convince the stiff-necked new vestry of its folly, he finally issued a pastoral letter to every member of the parish decrying the arbitrary, ill-considered behavior of the body in control of parish funds. In a single sitting, he averred, six men had undone the work of three years. The twelve-month battle that ensued is far from edifying. In the retrospect of a century, what didn't happen looks more important than what did.

Instead of yielding to the rector and the advocates of rebuilding the church, the vestry voted to sell most of the land still owned by the parish in the former burial grounds and use the proceeds to renovate the existing building. Renovation was to include the installation of a water closet and connecting it with the city sewer, extension of the chancel in a shallow arc on the east wall, carpeting the floors, fitting the pews with cushions and sodding the church yard. The outraged Dr. Lewis called a special parish meeting to fill two vacancies on the vestry and thereby obtain a less recalcitrant majority. For fifty years no one had dreamed of challenging the vestry's right to appoint replacements for members who resigned before their terms expired. Generals and admirals on and off the vestry were not accustomed to having their authority questioned. Was the rector now attempting to seize control of the "temporalities of the church" which tradition and law assigned to duly elected laymen? The rector angrily declared, and the Register admitted, that not more than three or four members of the parish ordinarily took part in the annual elections; although qualifying voters consisted of all white male pew-owners over 21 years of age, the vestry was virtually self-perpetuating. The upshot of the stormy parish meeting was the election of four new vestrymen by forty-four ballots, some of them cast by parishioners hitherto disqualified or never before concerned about who set secular policies.

Traditionalists, bothered by this break with the past, appealed to the Bishop to settle the question of who could vote, but the Bishop declared it a matter of canon law beyond his powers to resolve. In the course of the long-drawn-out fight over the rector's authority vis-a-vis the vestry's, several St. John's families transferred their membership to Epiphany Church. Indeed, a measure of the bitterness of the feuding at St. John's during 1869 and 1870 was the closing of the church for three months and the disbanding of the Sunday School for eight. Out of the melee came, however, a salutary change: a vestry resolution, which the congregation endorsed, whereby, irrespective of residence within the confines of the parish or status as pew-owner or pew-renter, any person entered on the parish rolls and contributing as much as 25 cents a year to the support of the church was to be entitled to vote at parish meetings. In slightly modified form a District of Columbia law of 1872 gave the arrangement legal sanction for all Episcopal parishes in the District; and not long afterward the diocesan Convention adopted the rule.

Fortunately for posterity, the newly constituted vestry and its successors did not resurrect the plan to rebuild the church at once. Common sense dictated first accumulating a sizable building fund. The rector, moreover, took a new tack. As everyone agreed that St. John's was too small to accommodate visitors easily, he and the vestry appointed seven "Trustees of the Building Fund of St. John's Parish" to promote the erection of a Free Church. An open letter to the city's church-goers outlined the scheme:

> No one, who knows Washington, doubts the importance of presenting the Church in its best aspect to the throngs of strangers and home-born, foreigners and sojourners, that congregate here.
>
> The need of a great Free Church, in this centre of national life, is almost universally conceded; and, from time to time, earnest efforts have been made to meet this need, hitherto without result. . . .

>   If a Free Church is to be built, an existing Rector
>   and Vestry must build it.

The letter ran on to assure potential subscribers that even
"if the New Church must be built chiefly by parishioners
of St. John's" at a cost of at least $300,000, the trustees
would guarantee that half the pews would be free to all
comers. Up to a point, the proposal had some resemblance
to the concept that would give birth to the National
Cathedral Foundation twenty years later and take visible
form in 1908 with the laying of the cornerstone of the
Cathedral of Saint Peter and Saint Paul. In 1872 not only
did the call for $300,000 fall largely on deaf ears, but the
infelicitous wording of the appeal made it pompous and
ineffectual. The statement signed by the rector that St.
John's "has been the Parish Church of Presidents and
Statesmen from the beginning," and the assertion that "No
parish of Washington, we freely claim, can be more trust-
worthy in such an enterprise" irked other Episcopalians.
Very well, their unresponsiveness indicated, let St. John's
handle it. St. John's couldn't.

By early 1874 an impatient rector and a committee of
the vestry had persuaded themselves that the parish building fund for enlarging the existing church had reached a
figure that warranted engaging a Mr. T. S. Cheville of
Washington to prepare new architectural drawings. A
"Prospective View of St. John's" tucked away in the
church archives chills the heart of the viewer in the 1970's.
Sketched in black and white was a massive stone and brick
building completely engulfing the original Latrobe structure. The porch and steeple of 1822 were gone. Latrobe's
lantern was scarcely visible from Lafayette Square, entirely
blotted out of sight from 16th Street by two heavy towers
that shouldered every lesser architectural feature into
obscurity. A ponderous square tower, like that still to be
seen at 12th Street and Pennsylvania Avenue on the one-
time city Post Office, occupied the southwest corner of the
"Prospective St. John's", a round, slightly less lofty but
equally overpowering, silo-shaped tower took up the northwest corner. Like the plan of 1869, Cheville's ran the
building out to the sidewalks and to the property's bounds

on the north and east. No drawing of the interior changes
has survived.

Economic catastrophe saved the parish from this mid-
Victorian architectural monstrosity. Financial disasters had
been mounting in Washington since 1872. When the ex-
travagances of a presidentially-appointed board of public
works assigned to modernize the national capital plunged
the city into virtual bankruptcy in June 1873, and when in
September a countrywide panic dried up the sources of
credit, optimistic Washingtonians had dared believe the
crisis would be short-lived. They were badly mistaken. By
the autumn of 1874 the business depression had deepened,
unemployment had spread, and suddenly impoverished
families that had never before known want were exhausting
their last savings. Every month of the next four years
intensified the suffering in the city. When the Congress of
the United States imposed a $885 tax on St. John's prop-
erty, the vestry was obliged to increase the fee for pew
rentals by 5 percent. That the parish raised $4,000 more
for its charities in 1875 than in any preceding year was a
triumph, but it siphoned off money from non-essentials.
Rebuilding the church had to wait. By the time money was
available in the 1880's better taste would prevail, and the
grim fortress planned in the 1870's would go into the
discard.

One unforeseen request dismayed the vestry in 1876.
The reestablished Lunenberg Parish in Virginia wrote to
beg for the return of the beautiful silver communion service
which Queen Anne had given the church in the early 18th
century and which John Tayloe had purchased a hundred
years later when the church collapsed. St. John's had used
the service for sixty years, but the appeal of the original
owners was not to be denied. By special subscription,
members of St. John's bought new communion plate; the
old went back to the Virginia parish.

Meanwhile the breach between the advocates of the
rector's ambitious building program and the group who
opposed it had mended slowly. Although Dr. Lewis's continuing complaints about the church choir kept alive a
certain amount of friction, it did not provoke animosities
such as split the congregation over enlarging the church.

The reconciliation came about chiefly through the increasing absorption of parishioners in the church's charities. In the autumn of 1870 the parish took on a new responsibility reaching into a field that neither the Home and Mission House nor St. Mary's Chapel could encompass, namely, St. John's Hospital for Children. For a time it was St. John's foremost philanthropy. In different guise, it would be its longest-lived and most significant.

The enterprise grew out of an undertaking begun in 1867 by several young women of well-to-do St. John's families who were eager to devote their lives to caring for friendless children. General Ramsey's daughter was the leader. Little more than girls, completely untrained, and living in their own homes, Miss Ramsey and her friends were not in a position to carry their plan far until, with Dr. Lewis' encouragement, they enlisted the help of older parishioners and, with about $1,200 in hand, leased and equipped a house on Pennsylvania Avenue. There St. John's Hospital for Children opened on All Soul's Day, 1870. Miss Ramsey took up residence; and one or another of her associates shared the responsibility a month at a time. The young women, banded together as the Sisterhood of St. John, soon had a varied clientele, ill children and healthy orphans, needy invalided adults and aged indigents. In 1872 Miss Ramsey took the religious habit and as Sister Lily ran the hospital with three other Sisters. But they needed larger quarters. In 1873 the managers of St. John's Home and Mission House offered them the use of a house on 16th Street, but as Congress had given the Sisters a $25,000 grant, they bought a very much larger building at 1908 H Street and transferred their patients there in December 1873.

The timing was all but fatal. The expenses of the bigger establishment rose just as hard times reduced the gifts on which the hospital had to rely. Sister Lily's death, followed by Sister Frances' in 1874 and the withdrawal of two others, left a probationer to manage as best she could. The humorless but determinedly cheerful Dr. Lewis reported in 1875 that since the hospital staff could not shrink further, it would inevitably expand. He miscalculated. By 1876 the hospital had become an unsalvageable casualty of the depression. Unable to meet the payments due on the property, the supporters of the charity had to find other homes for most of its inmates. Probably the aged and invalid adult patients had to find refuge in the city's overcrowded almshouse. The orphans, on the other hand, could not be abandoned altogether. Sister Sarah Huntington, a friend and former parishioner of Dr. Lewis, who had come from Norwich, Connecticut to Washington in 1871 at his earnest plea, took them under her wing. For months she drew heavily upon her personal funds to keep the children, while the managers of St. John's Home and Mission House contributed what they could. In 1878, with their help, she took forty-three children with her to an unoccupied house on 20th Street. There practically single-handed she created the home that came to be known in the 1880's as St. John's Orphanage.

St. Mary's Chapel fared better during the mid-1870's than the hospital-orphanage or the Mission House, chiefly because the Negroes who made up the congregation were at once devout and independent of spirit. They did not think of themselves as objects of charity but rather as participating members of a Christian fellowship in which all shared the burdens and the rewards. So far from being irresponsible and ignorant, most of them were people of character, possessed of considerable education and a wholesome determination to prove themselves good citizens and good churchmen. Mr. McKee, who ministered to them for several years while he served as agent for the Mission House, observed that men predominated in the congregation, a situation rare in any white church in Washington. Their responses to the services were so whole-hearted that Bishop Whittingham spoke of the lift of the spirit he felt when he visited the chapel. The first Negro minister, the Reverend Alexander Crummell, took charge in 1873 when the Maryland Convention awarded the chapel canonical standing. Dr. Crummell was a learned man, adjudged by contemporaries the foremost Negro intellectual in America. He had spent twenty years as a missionary in Liberia and returned to preach to his people in the United States that they must always recognize themselves as Negroes as well as Americans and children of God. The pride of race he infused in his flock benefitted both St. Mary's and its white sponsors. The latter had no occasion to adopt the patronizing attitude that often marred Negro-white relations. It was a notable example of the potentialities of a Christianity that, without fanfare, guaged people not by race but by what they were, and St. John's took pride in it.

St. John's contributed small sums of money yearly to St. Mary's, but the chapel's ninety Negro communicants bore most of the financial load themselves. Despite the severity of the economic depression, by 1876 the congregation had raised enough money to purchase a lot at 15th and P Streets and to lay the cornerstone for St. Luke's Protestant Episcopal Church. Three and a half years later most of St. Mary's communicants transferred to St. Luke's as members of an independent new parish. The remnant left in Foggy Bottom then came under the ministrations of "an excellent young colored man," Osmund St. James, who was a candidate for Holy Orders and whom Dr. Lewis appointed lay reader at St. Mary's.

St. John's Home and Mission House meanwhile slowly faded into the background as an operating agency. Although it was St. John's first major post-war charity, its functions, never clearly delineated, tended little by little to overlap with and then be submerged by those of newer parish organizations. Eight years after the Home's founding, Dr. Lewis collaborated with an Episcopal colleague in raising money for and setting up the Chapel of the Holy Communion at Virginia Avenue at 22nd Street, a stone's throw from the white St. Paul's Church and from Negro St. Mary's and in the very neighborhood where the Home and Mission House was endeavoring to provide non-sectarian, bi-racial social services. Tangential evidence points to the probability that, as the initial faith in the feasibility of bi-racial institutions wore thin at the close of the Reconstruction era, any charity that sought to combine help to white with help to colored people was doomed. St. Mary's succeeded as a Negro chapel; the Orphanage survived its financial struggles as a white institution. Mutual respect between the races did not add up to intermingling. The assistance which the Mission House, with collaboration from the Freedmen's Bureau, offered Negroes in the 1860's when Mr. McKee announced that the charity recognized no color line apparently became in the late 1870's part of St. Mary's program, while the white orphanage was the beneficiary of much of the residual resources of the Home and Mission. By a series of chance maneuvers the work of the Home among white adults merged with that of the white chapel at Virginia Avenue.

The Chapel of the Holy Communion which Dr. Lewis had helped to found had to close during 1876, the blackest year of the depression. At that point St. John's vestry, anxious to acquire land for a rectory near the church, arranged a real estate exchange with the trustees of the Home. The Home took over the property in Foggy Bottom at a cost of $3,000, the sum due for taxes, and in 1877 moved the cottage it had used as headquarters on 16th Street to the rear of the Virginia Avenue chapel. An assistant to Dr. Lewis then became minister to the chapel's communicants, while the Home and Mission House opened a workingman's club in the frame building at the rear. On the 16th Street lot thus relinquished to St. John's, the vestry began building a brick rectory for Dr. Lewis. The shift was sensible in many respects: the Home and Mission House was now located in the area where most of its clientele lived, while St. John's was able to consolidate its real estate holdings, install the rector in 1879 in a comfortable house a half block from the church, and build a parish house next door. But as the Home and Mission became increasingly an adjunct of the Chapel of the Holy Communion, it soon ceased to function as a bi-racial settlement house. Doubtless it had never achieved the complete color blindness that its first promoters talked of.

The multiplicity of undertakings which Dr. Lewis attempted to have St. John's sponsor produced a certain amount of confusion, particularly during a time when public and private resources were shrinking under the blight of the depression. A church secretariat was an unheard-of office. Record-keeping was casual except when rector and vestry engaged in battle; then the vestry minutes presented every detail in elaborately formal language. At best Dr. Lewis had more projects in mind than he could promote effectively or the church could finance. He resembled a

Don Quixote riding off in all directions at once. If his report to the diocesan Convention be a guage, in 1877 he himself gave way to near despair; he submitted the barest tabulation of activities: 46 baptisms, 13 confirmations, 6 marriages, and 13 burials. Although the vestry published three of his sermons, his gifts as a preacher were distinctly limited. Pastoral calls were apparently not his forte. While his persistent drive for what he believed in evoked admiration, he antagonized a good many people. He was earnest, not endearing. He tendered his resignation in 1879, withdrew it at the request of the junior warden, but a year later again submitted it. The vestry accepted it with expressions of regret. He left behind him a parish no longer rent by open quarrels but, nonetheless, uncertain about what direction to take.

3

A Golden Age

Affairs at St. John's in 1880 were uneasy enough to make the task of finding a new rector peculiarly difficult. Church attendance, already dropping during Dr. Lewis' last years, dwindled steadily; the Sunday School contained a mere handful of children. In November Dr. Frank Louis Norton came as rector but, because of ill health, resigned a month later. When the Reverend William Andrew Leonard of the Church of the Redeemer in Brooklyn accepted the call to St. John's in February 1881, a wave of thankfulness swept over the discouraged parish. Hopes were abundantly justified. Dr. Leonard infused new life into the church. Within a year every pew and every sitting was rented and a waiting list was growing. By March of 1882 the Sunday School had enrolled 252 children, and by Easter the parish debt of some $8,000 had been wiped out.

Some of this miracle may be attributed to the changes in the Washington community. At the end of 1878 the United States began to emerge from the long stagnation of business and the accompanying miseries of unemployment and want. By 1880 wealthy Americans were rediscovering the capital. The public improvements undertaken at ruinous cost in the early 1870's now bore fruit in making the city a national show-place. The imposing white or pale gray government buildings, the handsome red brick residences scattered about northwest Washington, and the broad well-paved

avenues lined with carefully tended saplings created an air
of affluence and spaciousness scarcely to be equalled in any
other city in America. Men who had made fortunes elsewhere and wished to enjoy the "season" in the capital
began to build here where they could entertain foreign
ministers and leading personages in American public life.
Scientists drawn by the opportunities to carry on research
in the government bureaus and writers who found Washington's unhurried atmosphere congenial added to the
varied interests official society offered. People of very
modest means still made up much of the city's population,
but money was not the key to a recognized place in the
social life of the community. Church membership, on the
other hand, was important. And what church had more to
recommend it than the Church of the Presidents? Inasmuch
as Mrs. Chester Arthur had been a member of St. John's
before her marriage, when the widower came to Washington
as Vice President he began to attend services there. In
September 1881 when James Garfield's death put Arthur
into the White House, the church on Lafayette Square
recaptured its title of Church of the Presidents.

The worldly eminence of the congregation, however,
could not have brought about the new spirit prevading St.
John's. On the contrary, many of the notables new to
Washington came to the church because Dr. Leonard endowed it with a special grace. The secret of his power lay
in his personal warmth, his human perceptiveness, and his
religious dedication. He was a descendent of the "thundering preacher" Peter Bulkeley of Concord, Massachusetts,
whose *Gospel Covenant* was "one of those massive, ex-
haustive, ponderous treatises into which the Puritan theologians put their enormous Biblical learning, their acumen,
their industry, their fervor, pathos, and consecration of
their lives." Dr. Leonard was neither a thundering preacher
nor an erudite Biblical scholar, but he possessed industry,
fervor, pathos, and consecration. He was, furthermore,
deeply happy in his work and in his family life. In language
reminiscent of the religious introspectiveness of an earlier
time, a passage in his journal written in 1883 reveals much
of his quality:

"With the closing year there are regrets, or a man is wrapt in his own folly; there are disappointments, and there is sin to be bemoaned. For all my errors I crave Divine forgiveness. But to me there is so much of full joy, so much love, peace, success, exhilaration of labor, so much to thank God for, that while I tremble because of so much undeserved mercy, yet my heart is full to overflowing with a consciousness of God's goodness to me and mine. I know full well how little I deserve any of this heavenly favor. Why is it that God will bless me, when I am so neglectful of time and opportunity, so full of hastiness of speech, so full of uncleanness and evil. . . . But I am amazed at His love and goodness, while I rejoice humbly, to feel that He condescends to use me as His instrument. I glory and delight myself in feeling that I may do anything for Him."

For all his self-examination, William Leonard was singularly outgoing. He quickly established close friendships with his parishioners. They turned to him for comfort in illness and spiritual travail and to share their pleasures with him.

The Rev. William Andrew Leonard, Fifth Rector   1881-1889.

Invitations to balls, receptions, and formal dinners poured in upon him and his charming wife. Although the social round was tiring, he believed that it widened his field of influence. As his admirers multiplied, St. John's inevitably became Washington's most fashionable church. If not everyone came to worship God, a great many did. Inasmuch as the rector and his wife had independent means, his $3,000 salary was not unduly strained in reciprocating hospitality. Poor and obscure people as well as the rich and famous were welcome guests at the rectory.

As church membership and the number of well-to-do parishioners increased, anxieties about the future of the orphanage evaporated. The orphanage had barely survived 1880; but for Sister Sarah's imaginative way of making ends meet, it must have closed altogether. Dr. Leonard upon his arrival promptly took steps to put it upon a firm foundation. He appointed a board of trustees, obtained a charter of incorporation, and in 1882 elicited a $6,000 appropriation from Congress. The grant enabled the trustees to purchase the house on 20th Street to which Sister Sarah had brought her charges four years before. An estate in Arlington given by one of the trustees, moreover, provided the children with a place for summer outings. As parishioners began to take an active part in lending Sister Sarah assistance, the Ladies Aid of the church undertook to raise an endowment fund. It reached $12,800 before the end of the decade, while an annual congressional appropriation of $2,000 helped meet operating costs. Technically, as a separate corporation, the institution was no longer a church responsibility, but the male trustees and the ladies of the Aid Society felt it to be very much an integral part of St. John's.

Statistics fail to reflect the quality of the household on 20th Street. Additions to the building during the 1880's bettered accommodations, and two or three resident helpers lightened the burden upon Sister Sarah; but people who kept in touch with the orphanage agreed that she alone gave the establishment its special character. Where the children came from is not abundantly clear. Often a relative, sometimes a neighbor, brought a child, and occasionally the police released a small vagrant to Sister Sarah's care; but ordinarily a committee of the Ladies Aid carefully investigated the background of each applicant for admission. When the boys and girls reached a suitable age, a system of binding out under indenture to responsible tradesmen, merchants, and private householders seemed to work well. The person taking a child had to be an Episcopalian and have the recommendation of his pastor. Apparently most of the children were reluctant to leave and always remembered Sister Sarah with affection. Thanks to her personal devotion to her "family," the orphanage was a home rather than an institution.

St. John's Home and Mission House meanwhile disappeared as a separate entity. After the board of managers moved it to Virginia Avenue and 22nd Street, it had fallen gradually under the aegis of the minister of the Chapel of the Holy Communion. The young man whom Dr. Lewis assigned to the chapel had succeeded in expanding its program and adding a building for a parish school, but in 1881 when the congregation asked to be set off as a separate parish, Dr. Leonard thought the plan unwise. Instead, St. John's vestry purchased the property and renamed the institution St. John's Chapel. Mr. McKee, who had served as agent for the Mission House a decade before, now became rector. By this process the chapel absorbed the functions of the older secular organization. Religious services combined with the work of a settlement house transformed the chapel into a small-scale "institutional church" such as advocates of the Social Gospel were introducing into New York, and Chicago, and Columbus, Ohio. The Reverend Charles Pyne, son of St. John's third rector, took charge of the chapel in 1887. He had lost a leg at the second battle of Bull Run; evidently never thereafter in robust health, he found the demands of his mission care too heavy. He resigned in 1890 and died eighteen months later.

St. Mary's Chapel, the other principal protege of St. John's, in turn underwent a metamorphosis. The transfer of the strongest segment of the original congregation to St. Luke's in November 1879 had left the remainder in Foggy Bottom almost wholly dependent on St. John's. White people accepted the challenge. From time to time the dedicated Mr. McKee added to his other duties a certain amount of supervision at St. Mary's, but it was two laymen of St. John's who started the Industrial School for girls there in 1881, and it was probably this Industrial School that was largely instrumental in revitalizing St. Mary's. A Sunday School, an Altar Guild, the Women's Guild, the Men's Brotherhood of St. Simon the Cyrenian, and the

Sunday services all attracted some Negroes, but the opportunity for girls to get expert instruction in sewing, dress-
making, knitting, laundry work, housekeeping, and cooking
brought families to the chapel who might never have come
otherwise. Initially the Industrial School met only on Satur-
days, but weekday classes and Thursday evening Mothers'
Meetings soon followed. Volunteers from St. John's taught
some of the classes, professionals the rest. The success of
the venture brought a small parochial day school into being
in 1883.

As the expanding work at St. Mary's called for more
space, a vigorous campaign of fund-raising culminated in
1886 in the construction of a handsome new brick chapel
on a lot adjoining the original site. The schools overflowed
into the former chapel. Dr. Leonard appointed a young
Negro minister as his assistant to take charge of St. Mary's
in 1888. The Reverend Walter Burwell endeared himself to
the congregation. Had he lived to carry on his work, he
might have taken his place alongside Alexander Crummell
as a leading Negro Episcopalian minister. Tuberculosis cut
his career short within two years and caused his death in
1891. As it was, St. Mary's served black people in the city's
west end in much the same fashion as St. John's Chapel
served white, but the wider range of undertakings in the
Negro congregation gave St. Mary's greater distinction.

Seventeen years after the junior warden had submitted
his plan for enlarging St. John's, rector, vestry, and congregation reached an accord on how to proceed. With the
number of communicants doubled since the mid-1870's,
tripled since the late 1860's, more seating capacity in the
church had become a true necessity. But no one wanted an
extension that would obliterate the intimate charm of the
existing building. Whereas Dr. Lewis had spoken enviously
of the magnificent edifices which other congregations had
been erecting in Washington and had pressed St. John's to
adopt T. S. Cheville's plan, towers and all, in 1883 the
building committee appointed by Dr. Leonard preferred
something simpler. An apocryphal story that had some
currency ran that Phillips Brooks, moved by the quiet
beauty of Latrobe's design, had written the verses for "O,
Little Town of Bethlehem" while he sat in the churchyard.

In acutality the idea had come to him when he was in Palestine in 1866, and he had written down the words two years later in Philadelphia and persuaded the organist at Holy Trinity Church to compose the music for the hymn. Yet the tale had an element of truth. The harmonious proportions of St. John's had an appeal that withstood temptations to accept the architectural taste of the mid-Victorian era. The problem was to find the right architect.

The choice fell upon James Renwick of the New York firm of Renwick, Aspinwall and Russell. Renwick had designed the first building for the Smithsonian Institution and the red brick Corcoran Gallery of Art; one indicated a love of the romantic, the other an interest in the stylized form of the French Renaissance. Renwick nevertheless immediately urged preserving the essential features of Latrobe's St. John's. He did recommend removing the steeple over the porch and substituting a campanile on the northwest corner, an arrangement which students of Latrobe's genius believed Latrobe himself would have adopted had he foreseen the change-over from a Greek to a Latin cross effected in 1822. But in 1883 the three generals, the two federal judges, and the admiral who composed the building committee objected to the change. The sixty-one-year-old belfry remained.

Renwick had married Admiral Wilkes' daughter and obviously had affection for her church. He showed real ingenuity in contriving to add 180 sittings without knocking out the north, west, or south walls. He extended the chancel to the east line of the church lot, placed an Ionic marble column on either side, moved the organ from the west gallery to the north side of the chancel, and adjoining it put up a two-story addition to provide a robing room and a study. A cellar dug under the robing room took a big hot air furnace and pipes to carry heat into the church. Relocation of the organ and the choir stalls left space in the west gallery for the new pews. A one-story addition to the south side of the chancel, a new aisle and new exit on to H Street, and some redesign of the fenestration constituted the other most noticeable changes. A Palladian window over the altar was above all an innovation, but deepening the windows in the west gallery and cutting new ones through the walls of the south and north transepts also made a pronounced change. The decision to install stained glass explains the need of additional windows. Plain glass shaded only by yellow roller curtains had formerly afforded more light than would seep through the blues and crimsons of Chartres Cathedral glass.

The stained glass made by Madame Veuve Lorin, curator of glass at Chartres Cathedral, and the windows portraying the life of Christ according to St. John and the Apocalypse, as designed by N. H. Eggleston of New York, were a source of peculiar pride to the parish. As these were well-suited to memorials, each of a score of subscribers gave a window in memory of a loved member of his family. Dr. Leonard and his wife gave one as a thank offering to the parish. In the north transept gallery one of two windows commemorated Presidents Madison, Monroe, and Van Buren, the other Presidents Harrison, Tyler, and Taylor. In the south transept was President Arthur's memorial to his wife. Other parishioners gave new altar furnishings. The Sunday School raised the money for the tile laid in the sanctuary, while the firm of Minton which made the chancel tile contributed it gratis. Renwick himself supervised the decor at every point — the coloring of the four evangelic symbols painted in the dome, the design of the oak furniture supplied by August Grass of Washington for the chancel, and the quality of the new crimson damask upholstery for the pews. Although the walls were painted a rather dark color in keeping with Victorian ideas of churchly dignity, the overall effect was extraordinarily handsome. The local press poked a certain amount of fun at the competition among parishioners to give the most beautiful and expensive presents, attributing their zeal to attempts to keep up, not with the Joneses, but with the Frelinghuysens, referring to the somewhat ostentatious Secretary of State; but the congregation was too delighted with the results to take offense at newspaper derogation. When the stained glass windows were in place, visitors to Washington thronged in such numbers to services in this exquisitely appointed church that the vestry engaged a corps of Negro ushers to seat strangers on Sunday mornings.

In renovating the building and beautifying the interior, architect, vestry, and building committee let no pronouncedly high church elements obtrude. Bishop Whittingham had leaned toward the ritualistic in ecclesiastical building and in the conduct of services during his 39 years as head of the diocese. Reportedly he had influenced church architecture in Maryland to stress the sacredotal and may have thought well of plans to turn St. John's into a highly ornate ecclesiastical structure. Bishop Pinkney, Whittingham's successor, put less stress on ritual. If Dr. Leonard preferred high masses to low, he restrained his taste in keeping with that of his parishioners. St. John's clung to low church practices. The architecture and adornment of the remodelled building still reflected Latrobe's humanism and the congregation's desire for simplicity. The one concession to people who longed for a touch of clerical formality was the introduction of a surpliced choir of men and boys, a change inaugurated in November 1883.

St. John's Church before 1883 Renovation.

"We live," wrote the famous surgeon John Shaw Billings in 1886, "in a fortunate time and place — in the early manhood of a mighty nation, and in its capital city, which every year makes more beautiful and richer in the treasure of science, literature and art." While devout members of St. John's no doubt wished the eminent scientist had spoken also of the place of religion in the life of the city, Dr. Leonard was aware at once of Washington's charms and of the quandary of the camel and the eye of the needle in this

pleasant urban society. Although he had turned a
disorganized parish into a
vigorous unified church
community, the rector's
unobtrusive stress on things
of the spirit was probably
a greater service to his
flock and to the city. His
very success brought an
end to his pastorate here.
After repeatedly refusing
calls to other churches, he
at last felt obliged to accept elevation to the epis-
copate. He was consecrated Assistant Bishop of Ohio in
October 1889.

*St. John's Church after
1883 Renovation.*

Dr. George Douglas, William Leonard's successor, inher-
ited a prospering parish with well-established institutions
and a modest church debt. Communicants had risen to over
1,200, and confirmations for the year 1889-1890 to 92.
The Sunday Schools for the church and the two chapels
had 54 teachers and 478 scholars, while the parochial
school and the Industrial School at St. Mary's had respec-
tively 3 and 17 teachers and 124 and 165 pupils. Generous

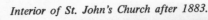

Interior of St. John's Church after 1883.

donations to the orphanage enabled the trustees to acquire additional land and enlarge the building where Sister Sarah and her small staff watched over their wards. The rector or his assistant minister daily conducted afternoon services at St. John's. Two other assistants took charge of the chapels. Indeed the parish was in such flourishing condition that the vestry saw no reason to hesitate over permitting Calvary Parish [soon called St. Thomas] to be sliced off from the northwesternmost bounds of St. John's. It was the sixth reduction in the geographical extent of the original parish since 1827. In 1891 St. Thomas Church opened on 18th Street near Dupont Circle; in the course of a generation it would rival St. John's in wealth and popularity among sophisticated churchgoers.

Stained Glass Windows, Made at Chartres Cathedral, Installed in St. John's in 1883.

Much of Dr. Douglas' time after his first months in Washington went to promoting the organization of the National Cathedral Foundation. Abandoning the plan which Dr. Lewis had proposed in the 1870's whereby St. John's itself was to direct the building of a Free Church, Dr. Douglas and other members of the clergy aimed at an institution that was to be truly national in scope. He

himself solicited many of the gifts
that made the Foundation possible; he
persuaded Mrs. Phoebe Hearst to meet
the entire cost of erecting the first
building in the Cathedral Close — the
National Cathedral School for Girls.
When the rector resigned at the end
of three years in order to accept a
call to New Haven, St. John's parishioners were startled. In fact, considered from a late 20th century
standpoint, their astonishment that
anyone would wish to leave St.
John's has a touch of naivete. But as

*The Rev. George
Douglas, Sixth
Rector, 1889-1892.*

least they no longer feared a long and disheartening search
for a new pastor. The Church of the Presidents, though
neither Benjamin Harrison nor Grover Cleveland worshipped
there regularly, by now commanded a prestige that should
simplify the task. Two months later the Reverend
Alexander Mackay-Smith began his nearly ten-year pastorate on Lafayette Square.

Alexander Mackay-Smith, well-to-do son of an old
Connecticut family, came to Washington from St. Thomas'
in New York where he had been an assistant minister and
the first archdeacon of the New York diocese. He had
abounding confidence in the power of Christianity, of St.
John's, and himself as its spokesman. A handsome man with
a beautiful voice and considerable presence, he expected
people to listen to him. And they did. As he had seen a
good deal of the seamy side of life in ministering to the
human wrecks in the slums of Gotham, one of his first
public statements to the press in Washington was an attack
on Robert Ingersoll's contention that "infidels" did more
for the poor and friendless of this world than did self-
styled Christians. Ingersoll, the iconoclast of his day, had
just lectured to a large audience in the capital and collected
a $1,000 fee. While the rector's sarcasm sounds more
labored than witty to modern ears, his diatribe against
atheism and his defense of Christian charity instantly won
him admirers among conservatives. In the course of the

next two years he was to have ample opportunity to prove
the sincerity of his concern for the underdog and his
conviction that the church must come to the rescue; for
hard times again swept the country in the autumn of 1893,
and, in 1894, Coxey's "Army of the Unemployed" arrived
in the city to demand measures of relief from Congress.
The challenge to a Christian society was clear.

Initially the new rector gave himself over to becoming
acquainted with his parishioners. His charming wife and
three little girls quickly widened the circle of new family
friends. But the rectory near the church, which Dr. and Mrs.
Leonard and the Douglas's had found adequate, was too
small for the five Mackay-Smiths and their servants. Dr.
Mackay-Smith's independent wealth saved the vestry from
any embarrassment; he bought a roomy house just above
Scott Circle on 16th Street. The old rectory then served as
an overflow for parish meetings and records. The rector's
house at once became a center for gracious entertaining and
warm family life. The day after Dr. Mackay-Smith took
possession on January 1, 1893, he held a New Year's
reception for "gentlemen of the parish," among them the
Chief Justice of the Supreme Court, Melvin Fuller, and
"many generals and admirals." Later the rector and his wife
began "to dine with the parishioners."

*The Rev. Alexander
Mackay-Smith,
Seventh Rector,
1892-1902.*

Like Dr. Leonard, the new rector kept a journal in which he made jottings of his social as well as his pastoral commitments. Unlike his predecessor, he did not pour on to the pages of his diary searching examinations of his own spiritual health. Very much the extrovert, he obviously believed that to do his best in serving the Lord was all God expected of him. And he enjoyed every moment of his service. Neither a profound scholar nor, as far as the record shows, a man assailed by self-doubt, he handled every problem that arose with a kind of contagious gusto. The upshot was an enthusiasm among his parishioners that eased their and his life. Differences between rector and vestry were practically non-existent. The nearest approach to conflict came about when Dr. Mackay-Smith discovered that some of the Negro ushers were accepting tips from strangers who wanted to be seated in the best pews on Sunday mornings. As the vestry demurred at dispensing with paid ushers, the rector issued an ultimatum: either volunteers from young men in the congregation undertook the duty or he would resign.

He dealt equally promptly with the more complicated questions of how St. John's was to lighten the material want in the city during the months of unemployment and business depression of 1894 and 1895. With the help of influential parishioners, he opened a coal yard at which indigent people could buy fuel in small quantities at wholesale prices. He organized a workingmen's club of which he had high hopes; General Miles, Bishop Satterlee, and the rector all addressed the group. As Dr. Mackay-Smith, himself a teetotaler, shared the opinion of many people of his generation in thinking the saloon responsible for much of the city's serious social ills, he started a Temperance Saloon on Pennsylvania Avenue. "It is like a real bar-room, minus the whiskey. No one knows about it, except St. Andrew's Brotherhood men, who manage it. It is so far fairly successful, more so than my coal yard for the poor, and less so than the ice water fountain at the Central Mission, where we gave half a million cups of water last summer." While these projects barely scratched the surface of the city's needs, each undertaking had the advantage of practicality and, coupled with the orphanage and the Industrial School at St. Mary's Chapel, added up to a program of charities on which St. John's prided itself.

As a wealthy man himself with a great many affluent parishioners, the rector was sensitive to the peculiar temptations to which rich people were exposed. Unjustly the newspapers at one point accused him of catering to Mammon in the person of the Cornelius Vanderbilts. As the Mackay-Smiths and the Vanderbilts were personal friends, the latter's wish to attend St. John's was natural enough, but when Mrs. Vanderbilt rented a half pew at a price of $1,500, the press carried headlines deriding the sale of Christianity. In actuality the owner of the pew, a vestryman's widow, sold the half space, just as St. John's pewowners had been doing at intervals for the preceding eighty years. The Washington *Star*, however, somewhat later remarked upon the earnestness of the rector's endeavors to scotch worldliness: "The Rev. Dr. Mackay-Smith . . . of St. John's Episcopal Church, which has the most fashionable congregation in the city, has been lecturing his flock for several Sundays past on the inconsistencies of lives devoted to fashion and society, with only the outward veneering of devotion to church-going and piety. . . . To a congregation which has been so long patted on the back, and which has listened to Gospel expositions without these stern, practical reflections on the duty of Christians, even if they are rich, the shock has been a great one and the west end has something new to talk about." Yet no amount of exhortation to focus on the lasting virtues quenched parishioners' excitement at having the wedding of Mary Leiter to the future Lord Curzon take place at St. John's.

At the request of forty young people of the congregation, Dr. Mackay-Smith opened a Wednesday evening Bible class to study the history of the Scriptures. That after two sessions 175 attentive listeners attended regularly, speaks for the interest the rector was able to awaken in a subject not ordinarily considered likely to engage the whole-hearted attention of debutantes and their beaux. The rector was also at pains to make frequent calls on elderly members of the parish, especially the aging Civil War heroes. He realized that in paying his respects to them he kept them close to the church; at the same time he found their reminiscences

fascinating. "Admiral Worden, who commanded the
Monitor, and who in later years was buried from St. John's,
has often told me," wrote the rector, "of the scene which
ensued when President Lincoln visited him after he had
been brought back to Washington. 'You do me great honor,
Mr. President,' said the badly wounded man as he raised
himself in bed, and Lincoln, with tears running down his
cheeks, clasped his hand and answered, 'The honor is with
me.'

"In later years I often used to see Adm. Worden riding
by my house in an old omnibus which passed up and down
16th Street. It was in this way that... he would strive to
pass the tedium of life when there was no longer work for
him to do. Back and forth he would ride from the Capitol
to the end of the Avenue, almost pitifully glad when some
old friend would talk with him about the scenes of former
days."

There were of course elderly parishioners whose anti-
quity and devotion to St. John's put them in an oracular
position. Above all, the seven McKean sisters fell into that
category. They had grown up in the parish in the 1830's in
a low church atmosphere which was subjected to some
strain when the high churchman Henry Whittingham became Bishop of Maryland. By the 1890's, however, the
sisters had recaptured their assurance. "One has always
done it this way at St. John's" was enough to settle any
question of procedure. Dr. Mackay-Smith, a middle-of-the-
roader in matters of ritual, once observed with a twinkle in
his eye that the Misses McKean were not merely worshippers at the church but made of it a religious dissipation.
For forty years they baked the communion bread, washed
the vestments, and scrubbed the chancel floor. They
worked altar hangings into which they sewed all the family
jewels – baby coral beads, some diamonds, and their
father's gold watch chain. When the last of the spinster
sisters died, St. John's lost a precious link with the past.

In 1895 the long-expected division of the Maryland
diocese occurred with the establishment of the Diocese of
Washington and the election of Henry Satterlee as bishop.
The rector of St. John's shortly thereafter became Archdeacon of Washington, an assignment which multiplied his

duties, but gave him an opportunity to foster interdenominational fellowship through a newly founded Churchmen's League of Washington. When the Postal Congress, "representing the whole world" met in the city, Dr. Mackay-Smith saw special significance in the fact that every member of the Congress attended the funeral service at St. John's for a delegate who had died during the sessions. The rector labelled it "the first time in the history of the world that all the nations of the world were invited into a Christian Church ... the whole globe constructively was present, and stood reverently while the Apostles' Creed was repeated!"

Twice within a single year noteworthy memorial services took place at St. John's. The first, honoring the late Queen Victoria, brought to the church President McKinley and a number of other American dignitaries along with officials from the British embassy. Dr. Mackay-Smith chose for the text of his sermon a passage from the 31st chapter of Proverbs: "Strength and honor are her clothing. She openeth her mouth with wisdom; and in her tongue is the law of kindness." The second memorial service, held in September 1901, was for William McKinley. The martyred President, a dedicated Methodist, had attended St. John's only rarely, but the rector's admiration for him gave the commemorative sermon a touching quality: "His religion was truly without ostentation, and yet, as I happen to know, it was the support of his whole public life," an estimate that a recent authoritative biography fully substantiates. "It is quite possible," the eulogy concluded, "that we may hereafter look back to these years as an unrivalled era of good feeling. The bitter passions awakened by the Civil War have largely died away... The President had the general respect and liking of the people of all sections of the country."

During the McKinley administration the families of Secretary of the Navy John D. Long and the President's secretary, J. Addison Porter, occupied the presidential pew at St. John's. Inasmuch as no President since Buchanan, with the sole exception of Chester Arthur, had regularly attended the Church of the Presidents, the pew reserved for his use had been assigned to any person he designated. The

St. John's Church, 1900's.   Harris & Ewing photo

congregation, as always, contained a number of people prominent in public life. Upon the outbreak of the Spanish-American War, a question put to Admiral Dewey asking whether he welcomed his assignment to the Philippines met with a response characteristic of many a St. John's parishioner: "My greatest and dearest personal ambition is to conquer Manila and to be allowed to live in order that I may return to pass the plate at St. John's." After Theodore Roosevelt became President, his wife and children occupied the presidential pew, although "Teddy" himself attended the Dutch Reformed Church.

The horseless carriage was still a rarity in the Washington of 1901. On Sunday mornings parishioners might arrive at St. John's in their own carriages driven by their "darky" coachmen, or they might hire hacks or take the rather recently electrified trolley cars, but a great many still lived within comfortable walking distance and came afoot. In mild weather to walk along the well-kept streets, to Lafayette Square was a pleasure. The square itself delighted the eye. Flanked by the White House grounds on the south, the dignified houses of Jackson Place on the west, on the

east the row terminating in
the former Dolley Madison
House (later converted into
the Cosmos Club) and,
along H Street, by the Arlington Hotel, the elegant
Clark-Freeman-Buckingham
mansion, the church, and,
across 16th Street, the
twin houses built by H. H.
Richardson for John Hay
and Henry Adams, with

St. John's Church, Winter, 1901.

the W. W. Corcoran mansion beyond, Lafayette Square was
an enviable location for any institution or private family.
And the leisurely pace of life in the capital, in contrast to
that of other important American cities, enhanced enjoy-
ment. Here in the heart of Washington, every person enter-
ing the doors of St. John's was conscious of its very special
surroundings. Neither Dr. Mackay-Smith nor, by all accounts, members of his congregation ever wanted to worship elsewhere. But the rector's talents denied him that
privilege in 1902. In February he reluctantly accepted a call
to Philadelphia to become Coadjutor Bishop of Pennsylvania.

Lafayette Square, 1900's.

4

The Perils Of Prosperity

In 1902 St. John's congregation, like most of upper class Washington, expected its world to continue along the lines of the preceding two decades. When Dr. Roland Cotton Smith of St. John's Church in Northhampton, Massachusetts, accepted the call to St. John's, Lafayette Square, the peace, material prosperity, and placid religious atmosphere which Dr. Mackay-Smith had spoken of as characterizing the McKinley era seemed likely to stretch on indefinitely. And outwardly for a time little change was visible in the capital. The city was growing; her cultural interests were widening; society was delightful and very much wrapped up in itself; occasionally chauffeur-driven Pierce-Arrows or Franklins passed up and down 16th Street. Conditions in the Negro alley slums were worsening, despite the efforts of the Associated Charities and the Sanitary Improvement Company in which Alexander Mackay-Smith had been interested. Foggy Bottom near St. Mary's Chapel was already a virtually solid black ghetto. Whatever the new rector's preconceptions about his Washington parish, he relied upon his proven gifts as a preacher to meet the demands upon him.

The descendant of Puritan leaders of 17th century Massachusetts, John Cotton and Richard Mather, and the son of an eloquent clergyman, Dr. Roland Cotton Smith was a preacher by inheritance as well as training. He believed that the function of a preacher was to guide the thinking of his hearers into realms which Christians ought to explore, whether or not social action was to follow. "To him," one parishioner later noted, "ideas were of the very substance of reality." He once told his fellow alumni of the Episcopal Theological School in Cambridge: "The School is not safe if all men are speaking well of it. It will be true to itself only if it is unpopular again, only if it is championing some cause that has not yet been won." He was of those "who in a complacent age felt the stirring of something new, who believed in thought growing out of life, who believed that life and truth are larger than any one man's conception of them." He spoke out sharply against cere-monialism and traditionalism as substitutes for a religion of the spirit. He was in no sense an orator. He was tall, awkward, and ungainly, and in the pulpit often did not lift his eyes from the manuscript of his sermon. When he gestured, he sometimes nearly toppled over the edge of the small preaching platform, until an anxious parishioner installed a wrought iron grill around it. But he held his congregation by the originality of his thinking and the force of his convictions.

Bishop Satterlee was undoubtedly grateful for having a rector like Dr. Smith at St. John's, for by 1905 the bishop was concerned about a changing atmosphere in the city. "A new type of residents are [sic] gathering in Washington,"

The Rev. Roland Cotton Smith, Eighth Rector, 1902-1922.

he wrote, "who, while they bring wealth, magnificence and luxury to the capital of the country, are, as a rule, actuated by no sense of civic, moral or religious obligation, regarding the welfare of the community." The bishop viewed apprehensively the effects of the careless irresponsibility they radiated. St. John's, though immune to an inundation of newcomers because of the long waiting list for pews, was subject to the somewhat different, but perhaps equally insidious, danger of self-satisfaction. "You can't get into Epiphany," ran a saying current in Washington, "unless you're a millionaire; you can't get into St. John's for love or money." Made up of families whom other people envied for their assured social position and long association with great figures of American history, the parish inevitably tended to be increasingly ingrowing. The newspapers repeatedly talked of the "exclusiveness" of the congregation and played up the worldly importance of its members, the impressiveness of the funerals held at the church, and the chic of the weddings. When Lady Maud Pauncefote was married, the throng of onlookers lining H and 16th Streets was so dense that the scarlet-coated, top-hatted coachmen from the British Embassy had to crack their whips at the crowd again and again in order to get the bridal party to the church. Gossip hinted that nobody could be a vestryman who did not command a personal fortune.

It was not of course parishioners' wealth and social distinction that threatened the church. But pew rentals priced in three and even four figures automatically limited the congregation to one stratum of society, and, insofar as members inhaled the fumes of flattery that implied they were creatures apart from the ordinary run of human beings, spiritual humility did not flourish at St. John's. Dr. Mackay-Smith had inveighed against the purse-proud. Roland Cotton Smith, with touches of his grim Puritan ancestry, lashed out at the haughty in spirit.

During Lent the rector conducted daily afternoon services at 4:15, an hour fixed by the 4 o'clock closing of government offices. The children from the Orphanage came regularly. Several hymns, a prayer, and a brief address made up the simple service. One afternoon, a parishioner recalled, after the hymn "Tarry with me, O my Savior," Dr. Smith

talked of "the great spiritual country" that surrounded the
material world, one of his favorite themes. At the rear of
the church a stranger had dropped in; he spoke to no one.
Several days later he wrote to Dr. Smith: "I had not gone
to church in many years, and I went in merely to kill time.
I was on my way to New York to put through a big deal
which was thoroughly dishonest, but would bring me a
large sum of money. When I got to New York I did not go
home. I spent the night on a bench in Central Park. Once
years ago in the African jungle I had a fight with a python;
it was nothing to the fight I waged that night, and I think
you will be interested in knowing that the Rector of St.
John's won." Some weeks later the man was taken suddenly ill and died in Canada. In his last hours he asked the
nurse to read him the hymns and the rest of that day's
service which he had noted down. And he directed her to
send his gold cuff links and the other few personal posses-
sions he had with him to Dr. Smith. The rector told the
congregation the story "because it does not belong to me —
it belongs to St. John's."

Reportedly the small Roosevelts liked to attend St.
John's with their mother because "the services were short."
When their father came, as he occasionally did, he joined in
singing the hymns with tuneless enthusiasm and listened
with interest to Dr. Smith's sermons. President Taft was a
Unitarian and rarely came, although Mrs. Taft and children
regularly occupied the presidential pew. In 1913 the turnover that put Presbyterian Woodrow Wilson into the White
House brought an end to the use by the Presidents' families
of the pew reserved at St. John's for the Chief Executive.
For the next fifty-seven years each President in turn attended
one or two services there during his term in office, but none
was a regular communicant. Each requested the vestry to
reassign the presidential pew.

Dr. Smith was less involved in community affairs and the
social life of Washington than his predecessor had been.
Lacking the independent wealth that had eased matters for
Dr. Mackay-Smith, the rector devoted most of his time to
his church duties, to promoting the building of the Cathedral, and to the Church Congress. As his wife preferred to
detach herself from parish activities, he bought a house on

Rhode Island Avenue near Logan Circle; the vestry rented
out the rectory on 16th Street. Two assistant ministers
carried various responsibilities; one of them took charge of
St. John's Sunday School. With no church secretariat of
any kind, volunteers took care of such routine tasks as
mailing out notices. Dr. Smith sometimes conducted services for the children in the Orphanage chapel, just as he
occasionally preached at St. Mary's, but Sister Sarah, the
trustees, and the Ladies Aid managed the Home. When a
fire occurred in the building in the winter of 1914, Sister
Sarah's presence of mind in forestalling panic among the
children awakened so much admiration in the city that the
Ladies Aid had little trouble in raising funds for a new
fire-proof building. Bishop Harding of Washington laid the
cornerstone four months after the fire. To much of the
parish, the Orphanage was second in importance only to
the church itself.

In January, 1917 St. John's celebrated its centennial in a
week of commemoration. No one present ever forgot the
moment when the rector asked the congregation to stand
while he read off the names of the famous people who had
worshipped at the church in the course of the hundred
years. A parishioner later exclaimed: "It was like a roster
of United States history." Dr. Smith spoke of St. John's
inheritance and made a moving plea for an endowment of
the church. One woman, deeply impressed by his sermon,
sought him out after the service to tell him that his elo-
quence had led her to a decision. "I am going to give
$10,000," she told him, "to my little church in Connecti-
cut."

Other events soon diverted parishioners' thoughts from
raising St. John's endowment fund. In late January Sister
Sarah died at the Orphanage after serving it forty-one years.
One of her former "boys" who had returned for her
funeral agreed to manage the Home until the trustees could
engage a new matron. As none of her assistants was equal
to the task, the trustees turned to the Order of St.
Margaret in Boston, which immediately sent two sisters.

War caught up the United States in April, and, later that
month, British and French missions arrived for consulta-
tions. The leaders of the British delegation headed by Lord

Balfour regularly occupied the British Embassy pew at St. John's during their sojourn in Washington. As spring turned into summer, young men of the parish left for military training and active duty. By early autumn men in uniform began to fill the church on Sundays. Parishioners eager "to do their bit" opened St. John's Rest House for Soldiers and Sailors near the Union Station so that servicemen in transit could have a place to sleep and get a meal when they arrived late at night. In the winter of 1918 the Federal Fuel Administration ordered two-thirds of the churches in the District of Columbia to close down for three weeks in order to conserve coal. St. John's was one of the few to be exempted, but the entire city rocked with controversy over whether the mandate was an interference with freedom of worship or whether all churches should put patriotism before religion. The Administration rescinded the order within ten days, but apparently few people remembered that central heating in Washington's churches was an unknown luxury two generations earlier. When word of the Armistice came in November, the bell at St. John's rang out announcing to Washington the end of fighting in Europe.

Like other churches and a number of secular organizations, St. John's took a fresh look at itself in 1919. The church edifice needed extensive repairs, and, in the process of arranging for those, the vestry decided to engage the firm of McKim, Mead and White, which had remodelled the White House sixteen years before. One change to the church's exterior consisted of adding four buttresses, two on the north and two on the south, with volutes of a 16th century style capping each. These strengthened the walls without obtruding noticeably on the main lines of the church. The other exterior change was the sealing of the two doors flanking the center entrance from the porch on 16th Street. The vestibule was then panelled. Four steps led down to doors on the north and south whence stairs rose to the gallery. The south stairs had been emplaced in 1888. Light cream-colored paint gave the foyer and the stair wells beyond a bright airy look. In the body of the church, marble replaced the plaster capitals of the two Ionic columns at the chancel; gray Siena marble lined the chancel

walls. A new wrought iron railing now set off the altar.
Repainting the dome and use of an off-white color to cover
over the stencilling of the dark brown walls, which had
seemed appropriate in the 1880's, transformed the church.
One agitated parishioner, having heard that the redecorating
was to be in "the Attic manner," expostulated: "The Aztec
manner? Why, the Aztecs were heathens!" Sight of the
white and gold decor dissipated her indignation.

The physical improvement was, however, only part of
the reappraisal the vestry sponsored. A specially appointed
committee set itself to examine all aspects of the parish in
1920. The findings were explicit enough. Cause and cure
were another matter. The committee reported 1,367 church
members. Of these 1,015 were communicants, 200 fewer
than thirty-five years before during Dr. Leonard's pastorate
and somewhat fewer than in 1914. Was the decline a
temporary post-war phenomenon or was it an indication of
deeper-seated problems? The Sunday School was suffering
from lack of teachers; the parish house, a dozen yards to
the north of the church, was more than roomy enough to
accommodate the pupils, but the dark woodwork and the
arrangement of the building gave it a somewhat gloomy air.
About thirty women ordinarily attended meetings of the
Women's Auxiliary. The work of the Junior Auxiliary and
the Rector's Aid Society was "satisfactory," that of the
Altar Guild "entitled to the highest praises." The St.
Andrew's Brotherhood was inactive. The organist, James
Dickinson, former assistant organist at Exeter Cathedral,
was a gifted musician, but he inclined to loose a volume of
sound deafening in so small a church as St. John's. The
Orphanage under the direction of Sister Cora was managing
reasonably well; Bishop Freeman thought it should be a
diocesan charity, but St. John's ladies wanted to keep it a
parish institution. Although St. Mary's Chapel probably
could not yet be wholly self-supporting, the committee felt
the congregation should carry a larger share of contributions to missions and parish assessments to the diocese.

All told, the summary was faintly depressing. In 1920
Warren Gamaliel Harding's successful campaign slogan ran:
"Back to Normalcy." But normalcy could not restore to St.
John's the position the church had held as late as 1910

before automobiles had begun to disperse the families of
the parish to relatively remote sections of the District of
Columbia. A downtown church was necessarily different
from a neighborhood church. Parents had to plan carefully
to deliver their children to the Sunday School when it met
before the eleven o'clock service or to fetch them if it
convened after church. To gather at the parish house for a
mid-week session of the Women's Auxiliary or to attend an
afternoon Lenten service meant a special expedition. On
weekdays there was the problem of parking. To survive as a
living organization, the church had to exert greater efforts
than ever before in its 104 years of existence. No one
seriously considered moving St. John's to another location,
as Dr. Lewis had wanted to do in the 1870's. Indeed within
the parish bounds, now that other parishes had taken over
the area to the east, north, and west, no site was better
than that at Lafayette Square. And the sheer beauty of the
church forbade thoughts of abandoning it.

As had been the case from the 1880's onward, the
church was always open during the day so that passersby
could drop in for meditation or prayer, but unlocked doors
meant that the sexton must always be on duty and had to
be paid accordingly. Everything, in fact, from coal for the
furnace to the altar candles and the sacramental wine, cost
more than it had before the war. Not only was a greatly
increased endowment fund of major importance, but a
method of ensuring a regular income throughout the year
supplementing funds deriving from pew rentals would be
helpful. Sale of pews by the vestry had ceased long ago,
since each owner bequeathed his sitting to his descendants,
or sold it himself if he left Washington permanently. Very
occasionally an owner willed his pew to the church, but in
order to have seats for visitors the vestry saw fit to keep it
as a "free" pew. As part of orderly budgeting for regular
expenses, the vestry finally adopted the "envelope scheme"
to encourage every member of the church to contribute
weekly, whether or not he was in church every Sunday.
Obviously, the sum expected would exceed the 25 cents
that had sufficed in 1872 to entitle a donor to vote in
parish elections.

Financial support, however, was not the sole factor bearing upon St. John's future. Like the vestry, Dr. Smith was aware that new problems were confronting the church. By 1922 he felt the time had come for him to relinquish his post. He had served twenty years, longer than any earlier rector except William Hawley. Pastoral calls had become increasingly difficult since the turn of the century. The scattering of the congregation through much of northwest Washington and over the District line into Chevy Chase had affected the close-knit character of the parish less drastically than might have been expected. Still, in the decade ahead, how was the church to maintain its influence in the community in view of the accelerating pace of life in the capital and the predictably greater turnover among residents? A younger man, Dr. Smith believed, could handle the situation more effectively than he. The committee report of 1920 had indicated that all was not well with the parish, although the signers alluded to "the affection and esteem which is felt for the Rector, by the Vestry and congregation, who so deeply value their relations with him as pastor and friend." Dr. Smith's resignation took effect as soon as the vestry found a successor.

One of the Articles of Religion of the Protestant Episcopal Church in the United States of America defines the church as "a congregation of faithful men, in which the pure word of God is preached and the Sacraments be duly ministered according to Christ's ordinance." William Leonard and Alexander Mackay-Smith had kept together a congregation of faithful men chiefly by personal relationships nurtured by pastoral calls; Roland Cotton Smith had concentrated on preaching the word of God. English-born-and-educated Robert Johnston, St. John's ninth rector, regarded ministration of the Sacraments as his foremost duty. It was also his abiding passion for himself. There was much of the mystic in him.

"For many years, immediately following confirmation at fourteen," he once explained, "I had experiences before the Altar which made me reluctant to leave the Church, unwilling to join my fellows, and unable to speak." Gradually he came to see communion as a means of realizing God's presence. "Great faith, great expectation, or great hope is likely to lead us to fruitful fields. In no religious devotion is this more apparent than in the approach to Holy Communion. If we approach it without expectation, we are conscious of no great boon; if we approach it in earnest desire, we are sure of spiritual help. In the sense in which it was originally said in the Gospel, it is true of the devout attendant at the Altar: Jesus is made known to men in the breaking of bread."

The Rev. Robert Johnston, Ninth Rector, 1922-1931.

Robert Johnston drove himself relentlessly to teach his parishioners the value of the sacramental life. He always preached twice on Sundays; at the evening service, after the choral evensong and recessional of the choir, he gave a Bible lecture in which he analyzed the meaning of particular passages. Scores of outsiders, many of them not ordinarily churchgoers at all, came to hear him. He looked upon the Bible as a record of religious experience, and hence of vital importance. "It is experience alone which can save Christianity today," he argued. "It is our lack of experience which explains the anemic character of Christians." For several years he taught a senior class in the Sunday School, and during Lent he always conducted a mid-week Bible class in the parish hall. He gave a series of religious lectures at Miss Madeira's School. His sermons, like his lectures, were thoughtful, and required close attention from his listeners. Not everyone enjoyed or approved of his insistent exposition of the inner core of religion. When the General Convention was revising the Book of Common Prayer, he spelled out to the congregation the reason for every proposed change, upholding the modifications of language because they restored the words to their original meaning. He defended the inclusion of prayers for the dead and, to the indignation of some of his flock, pled with fierce conviction for the recognition of purgatory. Its fires, "the invention of the merciful . . . are the purifying influences of a condition of life beyond the grave by means of which in time - shall we say? - we shall be fitted to enter into the nearer presence of the Eternal."

Dr. Johnston was intensely critical of a great deal he saw about him in the Washington of the 1920's. Just as he called the League of Nations "the greatest dream outside the Catholic conception of the Church, the greatest dream which ever hit the mind of man," so he warned of a "rude awakening to cynical reality." Such pronouncements startled conservatives in his congregation. His sympathies with his native England led him to say in describing the plight of post-war Europe: "England, remembered among other things for its great lead in the freedom of slaves, is chained for the moment in a debtor's prison, and is subject to poverty and loss." Here again were words that sounded strange—and uncomfortable—to many of the affluent Americans seated at St. John's, especially those who fully endorsed the United States' abstention from further participation in the affairs of Europe and rejection of the League of Nations. The rector spoke scathingly of the tittle-tattle upon which Washington society battened, never more so than in the post-World-War-I decade. "Our social climate breeds critical speech and this in turn tends to cruelty in words. From words we march readily to an attitude of mind, if not to deeds; an attitude of hostility which kills tenderness, kills pity and kills consideration."

One of his admirers observed: "In character, Dr. Johnston struck one as having a highly complex nature, with deep feeling hidden under an unfortunately brusque manner which made enemies . . . . He cared nothing at all for personal popularity; he detested all sorts of cant and what he called 'piosity,' and he took a puckish delight in teasing and shocking the stodgy. In the pulpit he became a different being—serious, intense and profound." With all his anger at the shoddy and pretentious, he felt an extraordinary tenderness toward his parishioners. "There are very few bodies of people that I have any knowledge of," he remarked, "and certainly no congregation I have ministered to, in which the spirit of religion is more generally widespread than it is in this congregation. The deep spirit of religion runs through St. John's in a manner that astonishes me."

The Orphanage and St. Mary's Chapel received little
attention from Dr. Johnston. Whereas every rector from Dr.
Leonard onward had kept a close pastoral eye upon the St.
John's Home for Children, in the 1920's priests from St.
Agnes Church took over most of that supervision. Every
Saturday afternoon, one or two cassocked young men from
that very high church heard the orphans' confessions. The
children apparently found the arrangement satisfactory, for
more than once a child exclaimed: "Father —— gives
peachy penances!" If confession and the accompanying
ceremonial of the high Anglicanism at the Orphanage
bothered any members of St. John's Ladies Aid, they did
not voice their objections to Dr. Johnston.

During Lent in 1927 the rector arranged with the vestry
to let the Rev. Florian Vurpillot, a French Protestant who
had married a member of St. John's, conduct Sunday afternoon services at the church in French. At Christmas that
year a volunteer choir gave a French carol service. As
nearly 250 people came every Sunday, M. Vurpillot became
the French vicar of St. John's. The congregation was varied.
"The number who came for a French lesson diminished
steadily," a visitor observed. "Yet a large number of young
people, boys and girls from eighteen to twenty-five, who
came because they were studying French, never miss a
service. M. Vurpillot seems to be able to catch the attention of the restless young mind. A large proportion of men
from government scientific departments are most regular."

"In addition to the services we have a French Foyer. Did
it ever strike you how hard it is to be set down as a
governess or maid in a foreign city, knowing no one save
the people of the household where you are employed, and
no one speaking your own language? This must give a
feeling of desolation, yet it happens constantly in this city
which, more than any other in the United States, has a
cosmopolitan character." Recognizing the tragedy of such
loneliness, M. Vurpillot planned a French fireside on American soil where strangers could make friends and establish
ties. "The Foyer is in no sense religious; one may be a
Catholic or Protestant without embarrassment, but must be
a member of a French-speaking nation—Swiss, Belgian,
French-Canadian or French. Many of the regular French

congregation are Protestants, but as many are Roman Catholics. Those who have abandoned religion in the past are encouraged to attend the services at St. John's. The 'practising' Catholics are urged to be regular at their own services. For these French services at St. John's are for those who have no Church."

Otherwise St. John's did not reach out into new fields. Philanthropic parishioners as individuals gave to various civic and charitable projects, and, as in the past, part of the church's annual budget went to support diocesan missions; but the church on Lafayette Square, so far from widening its activities, had narrowed them since the turn of the century. The coal yard, the Temperance Saloon, and the Workingmen's Club launched by Dr. Mackay-Smith had vanished with him. No one had attempted to revive a program comparable to that once conducted by the Home and Mission House. Interest in St. Mary's had waned after World War I. Although St. John's paid part of the chapel's operating expenses until 1928, when St. Mary's became an independent parish, thereafter the sums contributed for the sewing school and the chapel came chiefly from bequests left by St. John's parishioners of an earlier day. St. John's Home for Children alone endured as a major concern. Nothing in the church records indicates any questioning within the parish about the rightness of St. John's devoting its energies to St. John's. In 1928 the Washington Federation of Churches engaged a Negro sociologist to make a study of Negro housing in the District of Columbia, then, as now, a burning issue in the city; publication of the report produced no action. Community problems were problems for Congress and the District commissioners. In the 1920's few if any churches in Washington looked beyond their own congregations.

If the religious spirit which Dr. Johnston admired in his congregation and his indignant attacks on complacency and self-centeredness helped St. John's to weather the worst "perils of prosperity," the rector burned himself out in his decade of ministry to the parish. The vestry had engaged a secretary for him, but Mrs. Weech could not greatly lighten his load. His intensity of feeling, undoubtedly heightened by seeing the suffering in the city when the full force of the depression struck Washington in 1931, brought on a nervous collapse. At a time when parishioners acutely needed the comfort of pastoral calls, St. John's was left without a rector.

5

Responses To Depression And War

For fifteen months after Dr. Johnston's illness and eventual retirement, the vestry and the wardens had to run St. John's as best they could. Roland Cotton Smith took the pulpit at intervals, and other ministers filled in, but inevitably the arrangement was unsatisfactory. While the senior warden, Colonel George M. McClellan, son of the Civil War general, consulted with the Bishop of Washington and with Dr. Smith about who would be the best candidate for the vacant rectorship, a bold proposal came before the vestry: to allow women members of the church to vote at parish meetings. Women, after all, carried on a good deal of the parish work through the Woman's Auxiliary to the Board of Missions, the Altar Guild, the Ladies' Aid to the Orphanage, and the volunteers who assisted Mrs. Weech in the church office and handled a host of pedestrian jobs. Yet canvass of male voters' opinion brought in eighteen ballots against the revolutionary measure, eight for, and three in favor provided women were not permitted to hold church office. There the matter dropped. Colonel McClellan, who had been mayor of New York City at the age of thirty, later became a professor at Princeton, and served with the Army in the AEF before coming to Washington, used to say with wry humor that "New York politics with Tammany Hall was pretty bad, ... university politics was worse, ... the army furnished an even worse example," but that when he came to Washington and became active in parish and diocesan affairs, he "struck the limit." Much of the burden of managing the church fell on Colonel McClellan during 1933 and early 1934.

The vestrymen considered many possibilities for the post at St. John's before they finally chose the Reverend Oliver James Hart, then rector of St. Paul's in Chattanooga, Tennessee. Dr. Hart had served as an Army chaplain in the AEF during the World War and later as chaplain to the First Division. That phase of his career appealed to members of the "Army and Navy Church." In Chattanooga he had shared his pastoral and financial responsibilities with his wardens and vestrymen in fashion that strengthened the unity of the parish. His success there was a second reason for calling him to St. John's, inasmuch as the vestry especially wanted a pastor who would restore a sense of community to the geographically scattered and somewhat disorganized congregation. Born in South Carolina, Dr. Hart had kept many of the strengths of a young man raised in the rural South. With the clear understanding that St. John's was not to be a downtown preaching post, but the nucleus of that basic unit of the Christian church, a parish, he accepted the appointment in June 1934.

The new rector concentrated upon making and keeping personal ties with his parishioners. Besides bringing the church records up to date with the help of his assistant, the

The Rev. Oliver James Hart, D.D.,
Tenth Rector, 1934-1940.

Reverend James F. Madison, Dr. Hart spent his first summer in Washington in making pastoral calls. When he asked the church secretary for the parish list, to his confusion she held out the *Social Register*. "This," she said, "is what we always use." The rector promptly instituted an elaborate file system of pink, white, blue, and yellow cards according to parishioners' marital status and other personal data. "His," observed one of Dr. Hart's friends, "was a simple practical philosophy of Christian living centered around the parish church." Rejecting the idea that "the curse of the Church is parochialism," he insisted that "the curse of the Church is the lack of the right kind of parochialism." For the parish church, he explained, offered a continuing association of place. "Great spiritual experiences are not limited by but are connected with certain places." A familiar church, furthermore, provided association with certain people, "a divine fellowship joining life to life, and mind to mind through the generations." On All Saints Day in 1936, he invited his congregation to "meditate upon past associations." In looking back to former days, "blessed memories come to mind. We see once more the faces and hear the beloved voices of those whom we have loved long since and lost awhile, and these memories are a benediction." At the end of the service he spoke briefly but warmly of the lives of parishioners who had died during the year. At Christmas time he again called the congregation's attention to its ties with the past. The communion chalice used that morning had belonged to Phillips Brooks, and because he had made his first communion at St. John's on Christmas in 1857, Bishop Lawrence of Massachusetts, to whom Bishop Brooks had given the cup, now presented it to St. John's.

Dr. Hart's defense of "the right kind of parochialism" disarmed most critics. Those who hoped he would put greater stress on church obligations to the depression-ridden city could at least admit that St. John's Home for Children was in itself a considerable contribution to the community at large. Although the Orphanage was a separate, incorporated body, St. John's accepted full responsibility for it. And the institution needed help. In 1934 as financial problems were mounting, a crisis arose when a decrease in the number of Sisters of St. Margaret's obliged the Order to withdraw its two members from the Orphanage. The trustees succeeded in bringing in Sisters of St. Anne, but the rules of that Order required the Sisters to establish an autonomous convent within five years. Since Bishop Freeman of Washington refused to let a cloistered order manage the institution, in 1939 the Sisters of St. Anne also had to withdraw. A lay woman then became matron. After the outbreak of war on the continent, Dr. Hart was eager to invite refugee children from Europe to find a haven here, but no applicants appeared. As it was, the Orphanage was struggling to provide for its forty boys and girls.

Church finances and the care of the church property demanded close attention in the depression years. "These are not the things of the greatest significance," Dr. Hart noted, but while recognizing the primary importance of "spiritual ministrations," the rector and vestry were very much aware of the "temporalities." In 1934 the market value of St. John's endowment was about $50,000, but the precarious state of the American economy during the preceeding three years had led the vestry to neglect repairs to the church buildings. And Robert Fletcher, the sexton who had served the church since 1890, single-handedly could not restore rotting woodwork. The $4,000 given in 1934 for the missionary program of the diocese and for the national church came from a scant half dozen parishioners. Agreement that current expenses, including annual contributions to the diocese, should not be permitted to nibble away at capital funds, and yet that upkeep of the buildings was imperative, finally produced new procedures. Mr. Marcy L. Sperry prepared a series of careful recommendations of "deferred maintenance."

Adherence to this plan and several individual gifts gradually effected every needed repair to church, parish hall, the old rectory next door, now called the Church House, and the Massachusetts Avenue dwelling which the vestry rented for Dr. Hart and his wife. Installation of a sonotone system in the church improved the acoustics, and in 1937 redecoration of the parish hall transformed a rather gloomy room into a bright one suited to a "children's church."

Meanwhile a special committee drafted rules to safeguard the endowment fund. As a result, parishioners gained confidence in its sound management; within six years the fund grew to over $127,000. Anxious to induce more people to give specifically to diocesan projects, the vestry, furthermore, endorsed Dr. Hart's proposal to distribute duplex envelopes, into one side of which parishioners were to put their weekly contributions to St. John's, in the other their gifts to the diocese.

One innovation in policy had far-reaching implications. Upon the death of Dr. Roland Cotton Smith in August 1934, an old friend suggested that St. John's endow a pew in his memory, a free pew which visitiors might use without the embarrassment of intruding upon owner and renter. Inasmuch as estimates put the cost to the church at $4,000, the vestry at first demurred, in expectation that to obtain that sum would take five years. Eighteen months sufficed. In the interim, Dr. Robert Johnston's death and the vestry's wish to endow a pew in his name inspired several similar memorials. At the annual parish meeting in 1938, Alanson B. Houghton, chairman of the memorials committee, discussed the importance of this kind of gift. The thirteen free pews endowed between 1938 and 1940 marked the first step in what some people called "the democratization of St. John's," a project completed in 1963 with the decision to abandon pew rentals as the main source of church income and to make all seats in the church free.

In order to attract people reluctant to come to the crowded 11 o'clock Sunday morning service, Dr. Hart added a 9:30 service when pew rentals were not in effect. The early service enabled families to bring their children to attend the Sunday School while their parents were in church. At the same time the rector, hopeful of improving the congregation's singing, suggested that everyone who could do so stay for hymn practice after the 11 o'clock service. Later on, groups met in private houses for the same purpose. The audible results pleased everyone.

Convinced of the importance of sociability to the work of the church, Dr. Hart encouraged the formation of three new parish organizations. As the number of professional women in New Deal Washington and at St. John's multiplied, in 1935 he helped launch a Business and Professional Women's Guild. Its goals were to promote fellowship and open up channels of work useful to the parish and the diocese. Three years later the rector organized a Young Adults' Supper Club. On Sunday evenings it met for supper and then listened to a speaker discuss some lively current issue; periodically the members held a dance or a picnic in mid-week. Still more valuable to the church was the Men's Club started in 1935. When first proposed, it met with the objection from a vestryman that "there are no men at St. John's, and the few there are will not attend the meetings of such a club"—a pointed commentary upon the recent refusal of male parishioners to give women a voice at parish meetings. Yet when a Men's Club came into being, vestryman Alanson Houghton gave it a good start by holding the first meeting at his house; other members in turn followed that example of hospitality. While Washington gossip hinted that elegant surroundings and the hosts' bonded Scotch and Bourbon accounted for the fine attendance, the club fulfilled its purpose. It reawakened men's interest in the church, helped in recruiting men to serve on the vestry, and yearly took charge of the parish Every Member Canvass. "I felt," Dr. Hart wrote later, "that the Men's Club played a very vital part in St. John's during my rectorship." Adding that St. John's offered "a striking illustration of a church with an unlimited opportunity," the rector reiterated the slogan: "Put your money into men, not buildings."

In June 1940 Dr. Hart's resignation to accept the rectorate of Trinity Church, Boston, again obliged St. John's to find a new rector. The search was short. Tentative inquiry directed to Christ Church, Cambridge, in July brought the Reverend Charles Leslie Glenn to Washington for an interview with the vestry. The matter was settled then and there.

The Rev. C. Leslie Glenn, D.D., Eleventh Rector, 1940-1956.

Dr. Glenn's personal charm, his gay, witty turn of speech, and his professional experience as Secretary of College Work for the National Council and in a successful ten-year ministry in the Harvard setting banished all doubts of the vestry. He himself posed only one question. Since he believed totalitarianism was a threat to the freedom essential to Christianity and that pacifism was a "form of anarchy," in 1938 he had applied for a commission as a chaplain in the Navy Reserve. If war came and he were called to active duty, he would feel he must go. The vestrymen unhesitatingly declared that commitment no obstacle. "All would want to do their full duty, and the Church would want to be in the front."

So began eighteen months of a happy relationship between the new rector and his congregation. As the tempo of the national defense program quickened, St. John's prepared to meet new demands. Mrs. Francis F. Lincoln started a circulating library of books on religion; the thousand volumes were placed in a pleasant room in the Church House. Two secretaries now composed the church office staff. "The Leaflet of St. John's Church," started in 1940 and mailed out weekly thereafter except in the summer months, carried news of parish affairs and kept people informed of plans and progress. Robert Fletcher, sexton since 1890, took care of the entire physical plant until his retirement on a pension in the autumn of 1941. That year the vestry, aware that materials and workmen might soon be hard to obtain, had the interior of the church repainted, the pews repaired and reupholstered. The red damask for the cushions exactly matched that put on fifty-eight years before; it was woven on the same looms by the same mill that had made the original fabric. Meanwhile the addition of a kitchen to the parish house expanded the uses of the assembly hall — for informal gatherings over coffee after the Sunday services, for luncheon meetings of parish or diocesan organizations, and for special occasions. At the same time, the growing number of newcomers in the city who wanted to attend St. John's from time to time impelled the rector to appoint six head ushers with some thirty men under them to take charge of seating on Sundays. Without them an undignified scramble for seats seemed likely to occur, and elderly parishioners, finding their own pews occupied, would be inclined to stay at home.

Immediately after Pearl Harbor, while awaiting his call to active duty, the rector tendered his resignation. Instead of accepting it, the vestry appointed a three-man Executive Committee to watch over the parish in his absence. Fortunately, the committee could count on the help of the Reverend John G. Magee, who had returned in 1940 from thirty years as a missionary in China and had become assistant minister at St. John's. Dr. Glenn used to tell friends who inquired about his devout curate: "We divide the work of the parish: he provides the religion; I answer the telephone." When the Navy claimed Dr. Glenn in January 1942, Mr. Magee assumed much of the parish work. The recent death of his oldest son, author of a widely read poem *High Flight* and a flyer in the Royal Canadian Air Force, had been a crushing blow, but it enabled the minister to comfort families who faced similar losses. Younger men, one after the other, also served as assistants during the war. Dr. Norman Goehring left at the end of 1942 to undertake work with soldiers and sailors in Massachusetts. He was succeeded by the Reverend Howard A. Johnson who had been an assistant student pastor to Princeton undergraduates.

After Dr. Glenn's departure, the elderly and distinguished Dr. Howard Chandler Robbins, an outstanding presbyter of the Episcopal church, author of many books, and a noted teacher, supplied the pulpit as often and as long as his health permitted. "The Retread", he called himself. When he was no longer able to continue, two additional young curates joined the staff. One of them, James A. Pike, came three days after his ordination in December 1944; after a brilliant, brief ministry here, he would go on to become, in time, the most controversial and best known Episcopal bishop of recent history. Throughout the war, while ministers came and went at St. John's, committees of parishioners ran USO dances weekly at the parish hall and arranged other hospitalities for servicemen stationed in Washington or on leave in the city.

Franklin D. Roosevelt had crossed Lafayette Square to attend services at St. John's at the beginning of each new term before World War II. Bad weather and his own precarious health had then put an end to that practice. But on January 20, 1945, the privilege of conducting the special inaugural service before the swearing-in ceremony at the White House fell to Mr. Magee, Dr. Johnson, and the rector of St. Thomas. The second occasion for special services came less than three months later. Franklin Delano Roosevelt died on April 12th. That night beginning at 9:30, St. John's clergy held five unannounced prayer services; people filled the church. Hundreds more came the next day and the next. The church was never empty. On Saturday afternoon over eight hundred persons joined in a burial service that exactly paralleled the service being held at the same hour across Lafayette Square in the White House. On Sunday morning the Dean of the Washington Cathedral preached a memorial sermon, and that afternoon the French congregation took part in a memorial service.

Very different from the solemn tolling of the church bell during those days of mourning was the joyous peal that sounded out on VE Day in May. And, in August, when the capitulation of Japan brought the war to an end, the vigor with which three or four excited parishioners rang out the tidings broke the bell ropes. In November 1945 Dr. Glenn returned to St. John's. While he declared that the church had fared better in his absence than when he had been on the scene, his congregation dismissed his pleasantry with affectionate amusement. A long era of growth and new forms of service promised to lie ahead of the church.

6

The Church In A New Era

The years following the end of World War II brought to the Christian church the many-faceted problem of fulfilling its mission amidst the threat of atomic warfare, a worldwide population explosion, and, in America's cities, a crescendo of crime and mounting racial tensions. In the autumn of 1945, however, churches in Washington were able to enjoy relative calm heightened by a spirit of optimism. At St. John's, families reunited after prolonged wartime separation looked ahead, confident that Christian good will would rebuild the world. The immediate task was to forestall a wave of religious apathy and disillusionment such as had swept through the United States after World War I.

As a first step toward strengthening the role of the church, St. John's clergy and laymen undertook to revitalize the Sunday School. Gasoline rationing and war-time confusion had reduced enrollments during 1944-1945 to scarcely seventy children, many of whom had come very irregularly. Worse, according to an analysis printed in the *Leaflet* for September 30th, inadequately trained teachers, lack of parental cooperation, and a "vapid, secularized, unsystematic" curriculum meant that children were not learning the things "which a Christian ought to know and believe to his soul's health." To meet this challenge a new plan called for careful teacher training, classes for parents as well as children, and a three-part course of study arranged to progress from man's need of God as shown in the Old Testament, to God's goodness to men as revealed in the four Gospels, and, finally, to the character of Christian life as discussed in Acts and the New Testament Epistles. In order to enable parents of small children to attend the adult class and church afterward, a small staff of competent women would take charge of games and stories to occupy children of nursery-school and kindergarten age. The response to the plan was gratifying. After the first Sunday the adult class overflowed the rector's study in the Church House and had to meet in the lecture room in the basement. Teachers benefitted from their weekly training seminars, and the number of children in the lower and upper divisions rose steadily.

The return of Leslie Glenn, no longer in Navy Lt. Commander's uniform but now in familiar clerical attire, infused fresh vigor into every parish activity. Meetings of the Men's Club, dispensed with during the war, resumed; by 1948 the club had two hundred members. Further testimony to the interest men took in the church was the formation of a Men's Council composed of some twenty leaders in parish organizations. Eighty college students enrolled in the Canterbury Club; The Women's Auxiliary, the 125 members of the Young Adults' Supper Club, and the ninety-five members of the Business and Professional Women's Guild met regularly. One group or another occupied the parish hall every night of the week. In 1947 a Book Stall opened in the parish house basement where people could buy secular as well as religious books; the proceeds, at the vestry's discretion, went to the parish library. As the library expanded, a Library Guild developed from the library committee that had originally taken responsibility for purchasing and cataloguing the books.

If a cursory glance at the calendar of events listed in the weekly *Leaflet* persuaded the stranger that St. John's was mainly concerned with parochial festivities, a more attentive reading would show him that religious services took place at least five days a week. On Sunday there were frequently five, counting the afternoon service of the French Protestant congregation. Thus this downtown church in the midst of the hotel district offered visitors the opportunity to share in prayer services, to listen to the music, or to meditate quietly in a setting of peaceful beauty. And the rector was at pains to point out that, by 1949, St. John's had sent seventeen of its young men to seminaries to prepare for the ministry.

Unhappily, early in 1948, circumstances that culminated in Dr. Glenn's divorce the next year created a divisiveness within the church, which the vestry sought to heal by putting before a special parish meeting the question of whether or not to continue the rector in his ministry at St. John's. As a sizable majority voted to sustain Dr. Glenn, he returned to the pulpit on Easter Day after a three-month leave of absence. Some parishioners who disagreed with the decision, thereupon, affiliated with the Cathedral, but harmony, while less assured than before, again prevailed in the church on Lafayette Square.

One by-product of the distressing contretemps was a change in parish procedures. In 1947 the question of women's voting in elections for vestrymen had again arisen, but a reminder that male parishioners had rejected the proposal only twelve years before sufficed to postpone a decision. But, at the "town meeting," as one man called the special session of March 1948, women had voted as well as men, and the female ballots had not been thrown out. Thenceforward, there seemed to be no rational way of denying women parishioners voting rights. In December 1948 the vestry asked the diocesan Convention to endorse the change. It went into effect two years later.

Legacies enabled St. John's to finance a good deal of its expanding program in the 1950's. Although the pledges obtained in the Every Member Canvass, Sunday collections, and annual pew rentals covered most of the operating costs, as the total annual budget rose from the $20,000 of 1940 to nearly $80,000, income from the endowment fund was a necessary supplement to meet such expenses as enlarging the church's physical plant and contributing to the work of the diocese and to St. Mary's. Two exceptionally generous bequests permitted the vestry to acquire first a rectory and then a new parish house. When Captain James Edie, a lifelong member of St. John's and repeatedly a vestryman,

died in 1946, he left his entire fortune to the church. The
second major gift was the handsome house on Farragut
Square in which Miss Helen Sargent had lived until her
death in 1948. Conveniently located for a rectory, the
building needed relatively little remodelling to suit it to its
new purpose. The rector moved into his new quarters in
November 1949. At a somewhat later date one of the
curates also lived at the Sargent House. Negotiations for a
new parish house, a project made possible by Captain
Edie's bequest, were more involved.

The vestry had long had its eye upon the beautiful old
brown-stone dwelling which had stood on H Street alongside the church since 1835 and had served as the British
minister's residence in the 1840's. The walled garden at the
rear of the Buckingham house abutted on the north side of
St. John's and ran out to 16th Street between the church
and the parish hall. But while the vestry waited for the
settlement of Captain Edie's estate, the AFL-CIO bought
the Buckingham property to use in erecting union headquarters. A long drawn-out deal then began, finally settled
in 1954 by an exchange: St. John's released to the AFL-
CIO the lots on 16th Street occupied by the parish buildings and, upon payment of the difference in value, received,
in return, title to the H Street house. The architects for the
union headquarters and a committee for the church together agreed upon designs for the AFL-CIO building which
would preserve the dignity of the nearly 140-year-old
church.

Horace Peaslee, an experienced architect and long-time
parishioner, who had landscaped the church grounds in
1950, accepted the task of remodelling the Buckingham
house and linking it to the church edifice. It was a difficult
assignment, for church and dwelling were of different,
albeit not wholly incompatible, architectural styles. By
general consensus, moreover, the north transept of the
church was to be restored to its original form. Thanks to
Mr. Peaslee's skill, the passageway connecting the two
buildings neither marred the lines of Latrobe's design nor
prevented maximum utilization of the interior space for
such conveniences as the storage of vestments and room for
the Altar Guild to arrange flowers for the sanctuary. Below

the passageway was a place for the Book Stall reached by steps from H Street. The old house, four high-ceilinged stories and a basement that was to accommodate a dining room, called for installation of an elevator. On the first floor were an office and a kitchen, to the right two parlors, and at the rear the library. Studies for the clergy, secretaries' and business offices, and the Sunday School rooms occupied the three top floors. Although threatened collapse of the church roof demanded costly repairs, everything was ready by the end of 1955. On New Year's Day 1956, Bishop Dun dedicated the new parish house. Some of its handsome rooms contained furniture that had once stood in Captain Edie's house. Special gifts supplied other pieces. The church, repainted during the summer of 1956, now presented to the world exterior walls of a lovely pale yellow color.

Dr. Glenn announced his resignation just after Easter of 1956. His open letter to the congregation stated that he had accepted a post with the Mental Health Research Institute at the University of Michigan; he believed that a clergyman could make a useful contribution to the institute's scientific exploration of human behavior. After that, he wanted to devote himself to writing. His loss, one vestryman declared, was "a catastrophe." Even the rector's critics realized that as preacher and a powerful influence upon young people he would be hard to replace. The principal cost to the church, however, derived from a growing feeling within the parish of being adrift.

The universally beloved Frank R. Wilson, assitant minister since 1949, acted as *locum tenens* for nearly a year, until the Reverend Donald W. Mayberry of Trinity Church, Wilmington, accepted the rectorship in March 1957. Preparatory to Mr. Mayberry's arrival, the vestry purchased a new rectory on Bancroft Place, since the Sargent house on Farragut Square, surrounded as it now was by office buildings and traffic-jammed streets, was ill-suited to a household with children. The Sargent house for the next nine years provided living quarters for part of the church staff. In the interim, St. John's Home for Children closed; a careful survey undertaken in 1956 showed that as an orphanage it no longer had a function. What Washington in

The Rev. Donald W. Mayberry,
Twelfth Rector, 1957-1962.

the mid-1950's needed was a school for mentally handi-
capped children. Rather reluctantly the Orphanage Association leased the F Street property and, in a location on
Utah Avenue near the District line, opened St. John's Child
Development Center under the direction of Arthur S. Hill,
a man with wide experience in teaching the mentally re-
traded. The director of the Center and the new rector took
up their duties on the same day. Mr. Mayberry's warmth
and kindliness quickly won him the affection of his congregation. His tenure as rector, marked more by his gentle
pastoral gifts than by any dramatic new ventures, was a
time of consolidation, a period during which parishioners
grateful for the ministration of the colorful Leslie Glenn
early came to recognize also the special qualities of a
temperamentally very different rector.

The pre-inaugural service for the President-elect, in
January 1961, did not take place at St. John's, since John
F. Kennedy's Roman Catholicism precluded his attending a
Protestant church, but such disappointment as parishioners
may have felt was mitigated by the start of a new tradition.
In preparing for a commemoration of Lincoln's first coming
to St. John's on February 24, 1861, the organist found in
the church archives a Prayer Book of 1858 stamped "President's Pew." Church officials thereupon decided to ask the

outgoing President and former Chief Executives to sign the book. President Eisenhower and past-President Truman inscribed it on January 19, 1969, former President Hoover and Mrs. Roosevelt for Franklin D. Roosevelt a few days later. At the Lincoln Centennial service in February, Vice-President Johnson occupied the President's pew and added his signature to the Prayer Book, and Mrs. Woodrow Wilson, who was also present, signed for the President of forty years before. After Lyndon B. Johnson entered the White House as President, he would again inscribe the book; in 1965 Vice-President Hubert Humphrey would sign; and shortly after the inauguration in January 1969, Richard Nixon continued this presidential tradition.

Little more than five years after Mr. Mayberry's installation at the Church of the Presidents, the serious illness of

"President's Pew" Prayer Book.

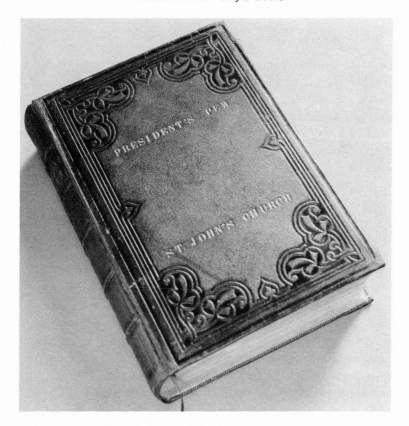

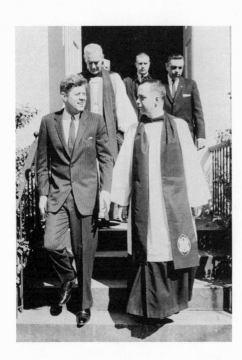

President John F. Kennedy and The Rev. John C. Harper, March 10, 1963. Washington Post Photo.

his wife forced him to resign. He was later to make a notable record as a missionary in North Dakota. While the vestry in Washington looked for a successor, the curates and guest preachers ministered to St. John's. Announcement ten days before Christmas that the Reverend John C. Harper, rector of St. Matthew's in Bedford, New York, would come as rector in February 1963 was joyful tidings to the parish.

Son of a much beloved Episcopal clergyman of Winthrop, Massachusetts, a graduate of Harvard and of the Episcopal Theological School in Cambridge, the thirty-nine-year-old John Harper had begun his ministry at Grace Church, Providence, Rhode Island, and, before taking the post at St. Matthew's, had been rector of St. Mark's in Foxboro, Massachusetts. His experience thus encompassed both big city and suburban parishes. He possessed strong spiritual conviction and deep feeling for historical tradition, along with an acute awareness of present-day problems and an engaging sense of humor. The growth of the churches to which he had ministered bore witness to his gifts of leadership. And he was blessed with a happy home life and a wife who took a keen interest in church and parish activities. Bishop Creighton conducted the installation ceremony on March 10, 1963. It had a special flavor, for, at its beginning, President Kennedy walked into the church to extend his good wishes to Mr. Harper; after congratulating the rector and shaking hands with the vestrymen and the sexton, he signed the President's Prayer Book and departed quietly, as he had come, by the side entrance on H Street. Eight months later, the bell in St. John's steeple tolled out for the martyred President. For twenty-four hours it rang at one minute intervals. The morning after President Kennedy's death, Lyndon Johnson came unobtrusively to the church for private prayers.

Richard Nixon and Vice President Hubert Humphrey Leaving St. John's Church after the Funeral of former Secretary of State, Christian Herter, January 3, 1967. Washington Post Photo.

Meanwhile testimony to the confidence Mr. Harper quickly inspired in his congregation was the return to St. John's of the parishioners who had withdrawn in 1948. He had made clear from the beginning that he intended to draw the church into the main stream of the city's life. A first move was to dispense with pew rentals, a measure calculated to sweep away the idea of St. John's "exclusiveness" and to pump new blood into the congregation. Some of the vestry initially were fearful of the effect upon church finances, and a number of elderly parishioners expected to feel like castaways with no place of their own on Sunday mornings. A few months' trial dispelled pew-owners' anxiety about relegation to an unfamiliar location;

they discovered they could sit in their old places by merely arriving early. Doubts about the budget vanished when returns from the annual fund-raising campaign showed that increased pledges more than covered the loss from rentals. Free pews furthermore resolved the difficulty formerly confronting husband and wife who had rented only two sittings and therefore could not have their children alongside; Sunday School children had had to sit as a group at the rear of the gallery. Now parents and children could attend as a family, with the result that the younger members could feel themselves truly part of the church. At the same time, *Education in Christian Living*, a brochure describing the Sunday School program, called attention to the carefully planned studies for children and the thought-provoking courses for adults which would run through the school year.

The Rev. John C. Harper, D.D.
Thirteenth Rector, 1963–

Fabian Bachrach photo

Respectful of tradition and interested as he was in St. John's long history, Mr. Harper nevertheless saw dangers in excessive veneration of the past. The church, he believed, must look forward, not backward; its vision must encompass the community, not merely the parish. In one issue of the *Leaflet,* he quoted from a poem of Edward Arlington Robinson:

We lack the courage to be where we are -
We love too much to travel on old roads,
To triumph on old fields; we love too much
To consecrate the magic of dead things . . .

"The unpurchasable man or woman," the rector reminded his parishioners, "looks into the future with confidence and with trust." As the time approached to plan for the sesquicentennial of the founding of St. John's, Mr. Harper proposed a special program totally unlike that of 1866 or 1916-1917. Besides a historical sermon Sunday, September 19th, and a parish banquet on the following Saturday, the celebration included a two-session symposium on "Church and City." The topics were "Crime, Juvenile Delinquency, and the Church's Concern" and "The Church's Role in Helping Our Community Meet its Problems." Among the participants were four clergymen, one of them a priest from the predominantly Negro Roman Catholic church of SS Paul and Augustine, Judge J. Skelly Wright, James Symington, then head of the President's Commission on Juvenile Delinquency, the president of the Washington Urban League, and the president of the United Planning Organization. If any St. John's parishioner in the large audience assembled at the Statler Hotel had secretly questioned the appropriateness of celebrating a sesquincentennial by such an exposure to current community troubles, the speakers' analyses of the challenge to the Christian church must have disposed of doubts. The past, however precious, was after all prologue.

Inspired partly by the enthusiastic reception accorded a superbly performed Bach concert at the church in the spring of 1965, another innovation marked the sesquicentennial. "Music," wrote the rector, "is an important and integral part of Christian workship . . .Christianity has always made use of the arts to express its truths about God and man." So, during the fall and winter, through the leadership of organist Phillip Steinhaus, St. John's shared its music programs with the whole Washington community. Three magnificent concerts offered Handel's Messiah and harpsichord pieces by Rameau and Scarlatti. Thus the past as well as the present entered into the historic celebration.

In 150 years St. John's had seen a succession of great
figures in American history gather within its walls. But, if in
the smaller and more intimate world of nineteenth-century
Washington the Church exercised a uniquely powerful influence upon the thinking and behavior of key men in the
national capital, in 1966, only the self-deluded could assign
that dominant position to any church. A paper written that
year by Senior Warden Russell Train suggested that the role of
the church on Lafayette Square in the decades to come was
not so easily predictable in a community where stability
suffered from the impermanence of its residents. The proportion of families in the congregation who had two or three
generations of association with St. John's had already diminished sharply. Diversity was now replacing the one-class social
structure that had long characterized the parish. To the
handful of Negro communicants in the 1960's the church
might add many more; indeed, the warden noted, they might
in time outnumber whites. Were the hotels in the vicinity to
give way to high-rise apartment buildings, the make-up of the
congregation would probably undergo other pronounced
changes. Out-of-town weekending, which for some years past
had reduced regular Sunday attendance, was likely to have
further effects; conceivably week-day prayer services might
become more important to church-goers than the centuries-
old Sunday services. Religion would certainly not lose its
power over men, but in the years ahead St. John's would
have to plan its course carefully if the church was to be a
vital force in the community. Still, the surest path to pursue
was, in John Harper's words, to "look into the future with
confidence and trust."

7

Looking Into The Future

To "look into the future with confidence and trust," as the 1960's drew to a close, required mighty faith. Men of good will had to fight off paralyzing discouragement, for, despite their earnest past endeavors, the evils they had struggled against persisted or worsened in American cities while baffling new problems arose — racial violence, angry protests at the war in Viet Nam, spreading drug addiction, and intensifying conflicts of ideas and ideals between the young and the older generation. Regarded by a good many young Americans as part of the "Establishment" that had created and perpetuated a greedy, repressive, and hide-bound society, the Christian church itself came under attack. Shrinking congregations and dwindling incomes hampered scores of city churches at the very moment when they needed larger human and monetary resources to combat the ills about them.

In January 1967, John Harper, after reviewing the first four years of his ministry at St. John's, outlined the plans he hoped the parish would endorse for the future. He ended with a quotation from Christian in *Pilgrim's Progress*: "I must venture. To go back is nothing but death; to go forward is fear of death and life everlasting beyond it. I will yet go forward." Aware as the rector was of the reluctance of some of the congregation to involve the church deeply in inner city affairs, he believed that kind of involvement

essential to moving forward. And because, under his leadership, parishioners chose to respond to the difficult demands
of the times, the church on Lafayette Square, unlike many
others in the city, grew in strength and influence.

An important instrumentality is setting St. John's upon a
new course was "Operation Outreach." Initiated in March
1966, it soon proved to be doubly useful, first, in helping to
meet needs of the community beyond the parish itself and,
second, in infusing fresh vitality into the 150-year-old
church. It began on a modest scale with the forming of a
"relationship" with the Chapel of St. Philip the Evangelist,
a diocesan mission in Anacostia. A first gift of $1,000 to
the chapel enabled the vicar and his Negro flock to complete the building of a parish house. Then, as interest in the
mission quickened at St. John's, volunteers from the church
helped launch Head Start classes and assisted with other
projects, while the vestry gave its backing to the non-
sectarian Frederick Douglass Community Center which St.
Philip's was organizing. From 1967 onward, the older richer
parish supplied the bulk of the funds for the center's
summer program, under which children from the Anacostia
neighborhood enrolled at the Potomac School for six weeks
study of Washington's civic history and contemporary problems. The results of the collaboration of church and mission were rewarding, the potentialities for the future exciting. The work tended to draw to the church young people
whose background and points of view were different from
those of most of St. John's staid and somewhat in-grown
congregation.

"Cultural outreach" also had an impact, particularly
upon people working or living near Lafayette Square. The
organ recitals given regularly by Albert Russell, the talented
church organist, had an especially wide appeal. Interrupted
during several months of 1969 by the installation of a
magnificent Gress-Miles organ, the concerts, when resumed
in the autumn, and the music at Sunday services were a
source of rare pleasure to diverse audiences. Following the
precedent of the sesquicentennial symposia on the church
and the city, St. John's furthermore added to its weekday
programs, seminars and lectures presented from time to
time by noted theologians and lay authorities on current

public issues. After 1968 another attraction was the series of contemporary films shown weekly in the parish house at the noon hour.

Nor was Operation Outreach confined to the ventures with St. Philip's and in the Lafayette Square neighborhood. It extended to a Visiting Fellows program that aimed at bringing three or four seminary professors to Washington every year at St. John's' expense for a fortnight's observation of church administration in a big slum-ridden city and exposure to the views of leading government officials on various nation-wide questions. When two years' trial led to the conclusion that a shorter period of intensive study would be as useful to the visiting group as the more elaborate and leisurely, but much more expensive, two-week scheme, the rector reduced the time span to four days. Some of the effort and money thus saved permitted the parish, in 1969, to tender help to the Star of Bethlehem Church, a Negro congregation in the Cardozo neighborhood, where a team of young St. John's parishioners served as a "technical assistance" group, advising the Negro church on business management and accounting for the operation of its day care center. At the same time the church on Lafayette Square established relationships with the Kingman Boys' Club, a new organization near Logan Circle, and with Voorhees College, a predominantly black Episcopal college in South Carolina. By investing $60,000 of its endowment in a housing program for low income families and $20,000 in a black, inner-city savings and loan association, the parish sought in 1970 to symbolize its spiritual ministry to the city by solid, material assistance.

Meanwhile, St. John's was becoming increasingly a training parish for seminarians and ordained clergy who came for a few months or two or three years, gained experience, and then moved on to assignments elsewhere. During 1967 alone eight students from the Virginia Theological Seminary profitted from the practical schooling made available to them through field work in the city and on Outreach projects, teaching in the Sunday School, and learning in discussion sessions with Dr. Harper something about parish administration. The succession of assistant ministers bore further testimony to the quality of the teaching ministry developing at St. John's, for, one after the other, they received calls to rectorships at other churches. The Reverend H. Vance Johnson, who had come with Dr. Harper in 1963, went in 1966 as rector to St. Christopher's in Lanham, Maryland, the Reverend F. Everett Abbott went to nearby St. Mary's, the Reverend John Evans to the Church of our Savior in northeast Washington early in 1968, and later that year the Reverend Noel Sokoloff accepted the post of minister at an ecumenical Community Church in Dublin, New Hampshire. The turnover sometimes seemed hard on St. John's, but parishioners realized that a pool of trained talent was invaluable to the dicoese and to churches beyond it. Able replacements, moreover, always materialized: the Reverend Peter James Lee came in May 1968 to take charge of the Outreach programs, while the Reverend C. Blayney Colmore III, successor to Mr. Sokoloff in 1969, undertook the pastoral work and religious education within the parish.

Several significant innovations marked the management of parish affairs after 1967. First was the inauguration of an annual Vestry and Parish Leaders Conference, an all-day session given over to scrutiny of parish goals, accomplishments, and failures. The conference was a useful device for ensuring a sense of continuity and yet encouraging the re-examination of policy. Another new departure was the

Interior of St. John's Church, 1970.   Anthony Hathaway photo

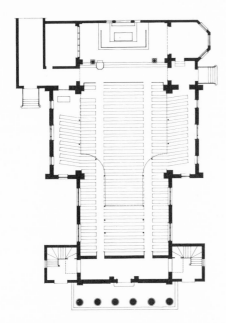

*Floor Plan,
St. John's Church,
1970.*

election of women to the vestry. Still another was the creation of a committee of laymen that met monthly with the rector to consider long-range plans; and similar committees met to advise each assistant minister. Manifestly, here were deliberate efforts to widen the participation of parishioners in decision-making on important matters.

One troublesome question was whether or not St. John's should continue to expand its activities and, if so, how it was to foot the bills. The cost of multiplying programs had already strained annual budgets severely; plans for a new organ increased those strains. And, but for the generous offer of Mr. and Mrs. Wynant Vanderpool, Jr. to meet the expenses of reconstructing the chancel, the parish would have had to forego that much desired change, desired because it would permit moving the altar several feet forward so that the minister could face the congregation during the celebration of the Holy Communion and thus restore the traditional arrangement that Latrobe had employed. Mr. Vanderpool, an architect himself and a vestryman, designed the layout and supervised its execution. Although the church had operated in the black since 1966, there was little or no financial leeway. Clearly, if the parish was to continue to add new projects yearly to its old, as well as carry its share of diocesan expenses and its own routine operating and maintenance costs, it would have to raise a great deal of money in 1969 and thereafter. The rector did not waver; he urged the church to accept the challenge. His parishioners followed his lead. So in the spring of 1969 "The Three Year Program for St. John's" was born.

The goal was to obtain $750,000 in pledges to be paid over a three-year period. Raymond Heffron, a retired Boston advertising executive and an old friend of John Harper, agreed to help organize the campaign, and a special fund-raising committee headed by Samuel Biddle, Hopewell Darneille and John Ferguson undertook to canvas the parish. Two pledges of $100,000 each gave the drive a big start, one from former Ambassador George A. Garrett and Mrs. Garrett, the other from Mrs. Arthur Gardner who volunteered to pay the entire cost of the organ as a memorial to her husband, the late ambassador to Cuba. The drive went over the top in less than three months' time. Elation ran high; at the beginning of 1970, the parish had a balanced budget in excess of $300,000 annually, the largest membership in its recent history, and its physical properties in good order. Dr. Harper saw the success as proof that his congregation cared deeply about the church. Gifts of money were a measure of what people believed in.

Del Ankers photo

The Rector, Wardens, and Vestry, Fall 1970

Not everyone in the parish saw eye to eye about what kind of activity fell properly within the realm of a religious body. Opinion divided rather sharply at St. John's on such specific questions as urban policies, race relations, and the war in Viet Nam. The opening of the church and the parish house now and again to protest meetings above all troubled parishioners who disapproved of identifying the church in that fashion with freedom marchers, anti-poverty demonstrations, and the "Mobilizations" directed at an immediate withdrawal of all American troops from Vietnam. Might not the situation, some members of St. John's asked, look like a confrontation of the Church of the Presidents with the administration of present-day occupants of the White House? Yet soul-searching that engendered a humility of spirit somehow enabled the dissidents to perceive that the church must minister to a diversity of people of widely diverging views. Thus, to an extraordinary degree, the parish not only avoided crippling disruption but attained a new unity. St. John's by 1970 had achieved greater strength than ever before in its long history.

Note on Sources

Most of the materials upon which this book is based are to be found in the church archives in St. John's Parish House. Especially valuable are the bound folios of vestry minutes, for years carefully inscribed in long-hand by clerks whose calligraphy ranges from an exquisite script to nearly indecipherable heavy black scrawls. Typewritten minutes cover the 20th century vestry meetings, albeit not always in the detail that gives special flavor to the earlier. The volumes of parish registers list, year by year, baptisms, confirmations, marriages, deaths, transfers of communicants from other churches to St. John's, and the removal of St. John's members to other places and new affiliations. Besides treasurers' reports and accounts dealing, often somewhat obscurely, with real estate transactions, there are a few architectural drawings of proposed changes to the church and parish buildings and some blue prints showing remodeling that actually occurred. A number of boxes containing newspaper clippings, photographs, mimeographed or printed folders prepared by church organizations such as the Ladies' Auxiliary and the trustees of St. John's Home for Children, and narrative sketches of St. John's of earlier days supplement the more formal records. In the last category Judge Alexander Hagner's account of the church as he remembered it from his boyhood days in the 1830's and 1840's is a unique contribution. Thanks, furthermore, to Dr. Robbins' diligence, a draft history of St. John's which he began in the late 1930's but never completed enriches the church archives, for he drew upon a good deal of scattered material, including diaries in private hands, and, equally important, upon word-of-mouth reminiscences of parishioners no longer living today.

Sources outside St. John's archives cannot be neglected. John Quincy Adams' *Memoirs,* for example, and Talbot F. Hamlin's *Benjamin Henry Latrobe* cast illuminating sidelights on the church in the antebellum era, and odd bits of information on the decades immediately after the Civil War can be culled from the volumes of diocesan records housed in the Library at the Washington Cathedral, although by the 1890's changes in the form of reporting reduce that type of parish data to meagre summaries. Interviews with the clergy and parishioners active in the life of the church during the last forty years fill in gaps and add color to the story of St. John's of recent years. And finally for the careful observer the beautiful church building itself, along with its skillfully contrived periodic architectural modifications, stands as a piece of living history.

INDEX